T0192402

Data Analytics and Visualization in Quality Analysis using Tableau

Data Analytics and Visualization in Quality Analysis using Tableau

Jaejin Hwang
Youngjin Yoon

CRC Press
Taylor & Francis Group
Boca Raton London New York

CRC Press is an imprint of the
Taylor & Francis Group, an **informa** business

First edition published 2022
by CRC Press
6000 Broken Sound Parkway NW, Suite 300, Boca Raton, FL 33487-2742

and by CRC Press
2 Park Square, Milton Park, Abingdon, Oxon, OX14 4RN

© 2022 Jaejin Hwang, Youngjin Yoon

CRC Press is an imprint of Taylor & Francis Group, LLC

ISBN: 978-0-367-74414-4 (hbk)
ISBN: 978-0-367-74416-8 (pbk)
ISBN: 978-1-003-15769-4 (ebk)

Typeset in Times
by MPS Limited, Dehradun

Contents

Preface

Overview

We are living with increasingly vast amounts of data through various platforms such as the Internet of Things, the Cloud, and Artificial Intelligence. In order to keep pace with the trend of this era, it is important to have a skill set that is quickly and effectively analyzing vast amounts of data. It is then critical to develop the ability to draw insights by understanding and interpreting the data. In this book, we will deal with effective data visualization methods using Tableau on the theme of quality.

Quality is an important factor indispensable in modern industrial society. Quality is a critical factor that is directly related to customer satisfaction and company profits. Due to the growing amount of data, it has become more important to identify critical factors that affect quality and communicate them easily to the audience. Tableau's data visualization tools will be able to meet these needs. We hope that this book will help to build knowledge and skill set for anyone interested in quality and data visualization.

Audience

For undergraduate and graduate students in industrial engineering, technology, business and management, and related disciplines, this book can be of direct help. Professional practitioners, including quality and reliability engineers, manufacturing and development engineers, managers, product designers, and marketing personnel can also benefit from this book. Anyone who wants to cultivate insights through data visualization can glean insights through this book.

Chapter Outline

In Chapter 1, we will introduce the basic concept of quality and briefly explain the basic functions of Tableau. We will also discuss how Tableau can leverage quality analysis.

In Chapter 2, we will cover various charts that can be effectively used for quality analysis. We will explain the basic theory and statistical concepts of each chart and explain step by step how to implement the chart through Tableau. Quality examples will be provided for each chart to help readers better understand the concept.

In Chapter 3, we will study quality analysis and data storytelling using dashboards. The purpose and basic concepts of the dashboard and techniques for effective storytelling will be introduced. We will provide examples of quality dashboards that can be effectively used in various industries.

In Chapter 4, we will analyze actual cases by applying the comprehensive analysis that we have learned so far. We will identify problems in each case and develop research questions to solve them. Based on this, we will create a dashboard by selecting charts to be used effectively. Finally, we will present practical implications for quality-related problems.

Text Material

In order to use this book, Tableau software is essential. Excel software can also be used as an auxiliary. Website links to the data used in the examples are provided in the book. The completed Tableau project file and associated data Excel file will also be shared.

Acknowledgments

Jaejin Hwang

Many people have helped in the writing of this book. First, I was able to get the idea and planning direction for this book thanks to Youngjin, the co-author of this book. I would like to express my gratitude to my wife Haewon and my son Jin, who understood and supported me during the several months of work. I would like to express my gratitude to Dr. Gagandeep Singh and Lakshay Gaba, who supported the subject of this book and provided generous and continuous support, as well as other staff members at CRC Press/Taylor & Francis Group. I would also like to express my gratitude to Dr. Purush Damodaran, Dr. Dong-Jin Pyo, and Matt Kroll for their invaluable advice.

Youngjin Yoon

First, I would like to thank my beloved wife, Bokyung, and my lovely daughters, Ina and Nara. And I salute the enthusiasm and energy of co-author Dr. Jaejin Hwang. We have different backgrounds, skill sets, and experience, but the difference makes a synergy so that this book could come out into the world. I would like to express my gratitude to the reviewers, Dr. Dong-Jin Pyo, Dr. SunHee Yu, Dr. Hyeon-Gyu Jang, who gave their insights for improvement during the planning. Lastly, I want to say that I always love my parents and families in S. Korea and the U.K., who always support me.

About the Authors

Jaejin Hwang, PhD, is an assistant professor of Industrial and Systems Engineering at Northern Illinois University. He earned his BE and MS in Industrial and Systems Engineering from Ajou University. He earned a PhD in Industrial and Systems Engineering from The Ohio State University. His research and teaching interests include statistical quality control, engineering statistics, reliability engineering, work measurement and design, ergonomics, and occupational biomechanics. He has published more than 50 technical papers including peer-reviewed journal articles and international conference proceeding papers. He has received a Bagam Paper Award from the Korean Institute of Industrial Engineers. He is an executive committee member of the International Society for Occupational Ergonomics and Safety. He serves on the editorial board of the journal *Work: A Journal of Prevention, Assessment & Rehabilitation*. He is a guest editor of the *International Journal of Environmental Research and Public Health (Special Issue)*.

Youngjin Yoon, MBA, MS, is IT Assurance Team Leader at Pitney Bowes and was Consultant at Deloitte with 10+ years of broad global experience (U.S. and Asia) in developing and executing strategies in alignment with business objectives. He has experience in diverse consulting projects for 25+ multinational companies with a successful track record of on-time and high-performance project completion. He earned his BS in Computer Science Education from Korea University, MBA from Washington University in St. Louis, and MS in Project Management from Harrisburg University of Science and Technology. His interests include business strategy and operation, data analytics and visualization, fourth industrial revolution technologies, and risk management. He is a self-starter, author, storyteller, innovator, and excels at leading teams by influencing, motivating, and delivering results.

1 Introduction

CHAPTER OVERVIEW AND EXPECTED LEARNING OUTCOMES

In this chapter, we will introduce the basic concepts of quality and quality management including quality planning, quality assurance, quality control, and quality improvement. Especially, DMAIC (Define, Measure, Analyze, Improve, and Control) approach will be described as a quality improvement strategy. The potential benefit of quality analysis will be discussed as well.

We will introduce the data visualization tool, Tableau, in this chapter. Several features and strengths of Tableau will be described. More importantly, the potential benefit of Tableau's application to quality areas will be discussed.

After studying this chapter, expected learning outcomes are:

1. Explain the concept of quality.
2. Explain the concept of quality management and related four major items.
3. Know the overall flow of the DMAIC approach.
4. Understand the basic features and strength of Tableau.
5. Explain how Tableau can leverage quality analysis.

1.1 BASIC CONCEPTS IN QUALITY ANALYSIS

What is quality? By definition of the American Society of Quality (ASQ), quality has two meanings: (1) maintaining the level of a product or service to meet expectations (of customers), and (2) a product or service that is free from defects. In other words, the concept of quality can be applied very broadly to our modern society, including manufacturing, healthcare, construction, and service industries.

When approaching quality from a macroscopic perspective, it is important to understand quality management. What is quality management? It means putting quality as the top priority in management. It is a company-wide, comprehensive management system that requires the participation of all members throughout management activities. The quality policy is applied to all activities in management to meet the desired level of customer satisfaction.

Quality management consists of four major items: (1) quality planning, (2) quality assurance, (3) quality control, and (4) quality improvement.

Quality planning determines an effective and comprehensive plan for quality based on documentation of quality standards, practices, resources, specifications, schedule, and framework. It gives an overall direction of what to do.

Quality assurance refers to all planned and systematic activities carried out in the quality system to give an appropriate sense of confidence that the product or service meets quality requirements.

Quality control refers to operational techniques and activities used to meet quality requirements. Quality control can be considered as a sub-concept of quality assurance. Quality assurance is an activity that places a lot of weight on the customer's point of view and taking more comprehensive responsibility for the product. On the other hand, quality control puts a lot of weight on the product and verifies the function according to the specifications of the product (Figure 1.1).

Quality improvement focuses on improving the performance of products or services. The PDSA (plan-do-study-act) cycles are commonly used approaches. In these PDSA cycles, quality personnel try and test new improvement methods through iterative cycles until they feel confident of implementing them for the desired results. PDSA is also called the Deming Cycle. Dr. W. Edward Deming is known as the "father" of the field of quality management. The core of PDSA is that when improving quality problems, it is necessary to pay attention to the overall system and process with a long-term perspective rather than urgently taking care of the problems in front. Deming emphasized that the quality problem is not a fault of field workers, but rather a problem of the part of the manager's responsibility or the entire system.

For quality improvement, the Define, Measure, Analyze, Improve, and Control (DMAIC) is another well-known quality strategy to improve the entire process. As the name stated, this strategy consists of five phases. This strategy could be widely applied to any standard quality improvement procedure. Figure 1.2 shows the flow chart of the DMAIC methodology (Ansar et al., 2018).

- Define
  In this stage, the problem of the process is defined, and the related project scope is determined. The project goals and customers' expectations are clearly defined. This stage is important to determine the overall direction of

FIGURE 1.1   Quality management, quality assurance, and quality control relationships.

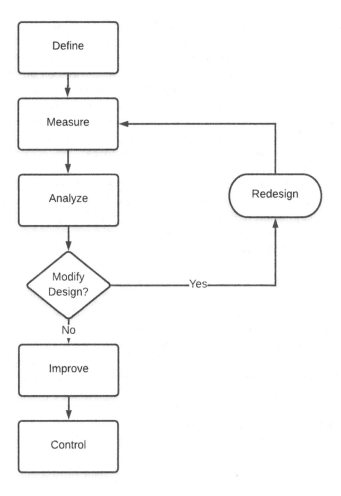

FIGURE 1.2   The flow chart of the DMAIC methodology.

the project. To better define the project, the voice of the customer and value
stream map could be considered to understand the customers' expectations
and the overall flow of the entire process.

- Measure
  This stage directly measures the performance of the process. Process map
  (i.e., flow chart) can be used to document each operation (i.e., activity) under
  the process. Process capability analysis can be considered to assess whether
  the inherent variability of the process meets the specification limits which are
  externally determined. The Pareto chart is another useful tool to extract a few
  significant vital factors affecting the overall quality of the process.

- Analyze
  This stage analyses the process to find out the root causes of the low performance of the process. The root cause analysis (e.g., cause-and-effect diagram)
  could be considered to brainstorm and summarize potential causes of the

quality issues. The Failure Model and Effects Analysis (FMES) could be useful to identify and prioritize the potential failures (e.g., defects) of the process based on the severity, expected frequency, and the probability of detection. The multi-vari chart is another useful tool to assess the variation of multiple operations in the process. After analyzing various methods, it could be determined whether the redesign of the process is necessary. If the modification of the design is necessary, it can go back to the Measure stage to evaluate the quality characteristics of the redesigned process. If there is no need for the modification, it can move forward to the next step, Improve.

- Improve

  This stage addresses the assignable causes of the issues to improve the quality of the process. The design of experiment methodology could be considered to identify key factors critically affecting the quality or performance of the process. Once major factors are identified, improvement efforts could be prioritized on these factors.

- Control

  Once the process is improved by eliminating the issues, this stage controls and maintains the improved performance of the process. A quality control plan could be initially designed and documented to consider several quality-related resources such as quality standards, practices, specifications, and contracts. After that, statistical process control charts could be used to monitor the quality characteristics of the process. This approach helps to identify unusual events such as very high or low process variation. The five S (5S: sort, set in order, shine, standardize, sustain) could also help to organize the workplace and better control the process.

  Within the quality management system, the above-mentioned factors should be improved and evolved in a continuous improvement cycle, as seen in Figure 1.3.

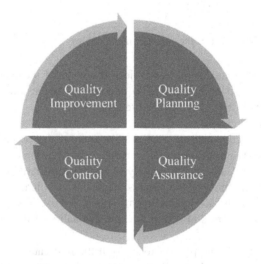

FIGURE 1.3   Quality management cycle.

Jack Welch of General Electric (GE) firmly believed that quality control could be the critical factor in making companies most competitive and meeting customer satisfaction. Jack Welch operated the 'Six Sigma' program and performed the DMAIC steps. All GE employees have been involved in this process, and this program substantially reduced the defective rate of the products. Because of his rigorous quality management system, in the 20 years of his tenure as CEO, sales have increased fivefold. Quality management levels may differ depending on the degree of practice or implementation method, the interest of top management, corporate size, and culture, but in general, the following effects can be expected through quality management.

- Cost reduction
  The quality analysis helps to identify the waste in the process. The reduction of waste directly affects the cost reduction in the product development stage. Increased quality of the product also reduces the occurrences of repairs, which lowers the cost of fixing the product.
- Improved brand reputation
  If customers experience a good quality of the product or service, they trust more about the company. Customers could feel more favorable about purchasing the items from the company.
- Better customer experience
  The quality analysis helps to determine the critical factors affecting the customers' experience and satisfaction. This information is useful to improve the system and the end product to meet customers' expectations.
- Increased revenue
  The aforementioned cost reduction due to the quality analysis is directly related to increased revenue. Increased sales because of the good quality of products could lead to greater revenue.

1.2   WHAT IS TABLEAU?

Looking at the background behind the Tableau company's founders, the core goal of the software can be understood more clearly. Tableau is a company founded by three Stanford University graduates Christian, Chris, and Pat. They were working on a data analysis project in 1999, and they had a hard time running the program using Business intelligence (BI) software commonly used in the market. Even those who majored in subjects related to computers had difficulty operating BI software. They realized the need for improvement in BI software. Through this, the Tableau Company was founded in 2003, and the main management philosophy is "Helping people see and understand data." In other words, Tableau is a leading analytics platform company that allows anyone, regardless of skill level, to use and work with data.

Tableau Software is one of the fastest-growing data visualization tools which helps people to view and understand the characteristics of data. It involves intuitive and spontaneous user interface technologies such as dragging and dropping interactions, which makes it easy for users to learn and use the tool. Interactive visualizations, including graphs, dashboards, maps, and tables, encourage users to build their customized visualization reports.

Any type and size of data can be connected, analyzed, and visualized through Tableau. We can interpret and understand the results by collecting, storing, and analyzing data through Tableau. Based on the results of the analysis, we can come up with the processes and methods that optimize the desired outcomes in studies or business. In other words, it aims to use data to make the best decisions and, as a result, to get an optimal solution to achieve the desired goal.

In the past, gathering, connecting, analyzing, and understanding data was not a simple task. It required a high level of technical knowledge such as Structured Query Language, Relational Database, Statistics, and so on. Therefore, since collaboration with the IT department or data experts was essential in order to utilize the data, there was a clear limit to the slow processing speed or the accuracy of data interpretation.

With the advent of the data visualization tool, Tableau, users minimize their dependence on the IT department or data experts when analyzing data and it helps users analyze, interpret, and understand the data themselves. Through this, end users can gather, connect, analyze, and understand data and discover insights through constant repetition of questions and answers to achieve goals.

As a result, Tableau helps organizations or individuals use data in the area of self-service analysis, where they see and understand data by themselves. Currently, Tableau is a trusted leader in data analytics, helping people and organizations to make more data-driven decisions.

In this book, the Tableau Desktop version will be used for all examples. Tableau Desktop provides an environment where we can directly connect and analyze data sources stored on-premises or in the cloud. Users can view and understand data with just drag, drop, and double click. Furthermore, it provides an environment in which data can be viewed interactively through a dashboard. Advanced analysis is also possible by using additional functions such as various calculation functions, line addition, and data clustering. If necessary, Tableau Server/Online or Tableau Prep provided by Tableau can be used to take advantage of additional features.

Tableau offers a 14-day free trial to anyone interested in Tableau. (https://www.tableau.com/products/trial). If the user is a student or faculty member of an accredited educational institution, it can be used for free with a one-year free license for Academic (renewable for enrolled students). Download Tableau through the following link (https://www.tableau.com/academic) and upload your personal information, student ID card, transcript, and enrollment certificate, and you can use the Academic version after verification of the documents. Tableau also provides a free version, Tableau Public. Although there are some limitations, including the connectors, security, and data source capacity, all the examples in this book can be easily practiced in Tableau Public (https://public.tableau.com/en-us/s/download).

1.3 HOW TO LEVERAGE TABLEAU IN QUALITY ANALYSIS

When performing quality analysis, there are many cases where we may come across vast amounts of data related to manufacturing, construction, healthcare, or service industries. In this case, we mainly rely on Excel or statistical analysis software such as Minitab, SPSS, SAS, JMP, and R. Effective handling of such a large amount of data often requires expert knowledge of statistics or the skill set of advanced Excel functions.

Using Tableau, a data visualization tool, could lower the barriers to entry for using vast amounts of data. For example, Tableau helps you visualize and analyze massive amounts of data in a variety of ways through simple interaction functions such as dragging and dropping. When performing quality analysis, there are cases where the data contains various categories of information, such as part number, customer type, department, or location. In this situation, the intuitive use of Tableau can reduce the analyst's time and effort, and motive users to try a variety of creative approaches to deeply understand the data.

Chapter 2 will cover some of the Tableau charts that are useful for quality analysis. We will first introduce the basic or statistical concepts of various charts and show how to create charts in Tableau by giving step-by-step instructions. In Chapter 3, we will focus on the dashboard, which is a presentation method that effectively conveys the overall data result by collecting several charts. It will introduce some of the techniques and visualization tips for creating dashboards effectively. Finally, in Chapter 4, we will share the process of solving problems using Tableau based on real data related to quality. Based on the knowledge of the charts and dashboards learned in the previous chapters, we can discern which charts can be effectively used to understand the quality characteristics of each case study.

REFERENCE

Ansar, A. R., Shaju, S. U. C., Sarkar, S. K., Hashem, M. Z., Hasan, S. K., & Islam, U. (2018). Application of six sigma using define measure analyze improve control (DMAIC) methodology in garment sector. *Independent Journal of Management & Production*, 9(3), 810–826. Instituto Federal de Educação, Ciência e Tecnologia de São Paulo (IFSP).

2 Basic Quality Tools with Tableau

CHAPTER OVERVIEW AND EXPECTED LEARNING OUTCOMES

In this chapter, we will introduce several charts that could be effectively used in quality analysis. For some charts that require a basic understanding of statistics, the relevant statistical theory will be provided with an example. For each chart, step-by-step instructions of using Tableau will be provided. More detailed procedures of using Tableau will be given at the beginning, and more concise instructions of using Tableau will be shown later to minimize the duplication. Some example data will be used from open datasets. In that case, a reference link will be provided for accessing the full dataset.

After studying this chapter, expected learning outcomes are:

1. Explain the basic concepts of the chart.
2. Know how to use Tableau for constructing charts.
3. Understand statistical concepts behind the charts.
4. Interpret the chart results rooted in the quality concept.

WHAT IS THE CHART?

There is a phrase that emphasizes the importance of the chart, "A Picture is Worth a Thousand Words." This is closely related to our brain's ability to process information. The human brain concentrates through attentive processing when reading text, but when viewing a visual picture (i.e., chart), it absorbs information in an intuitive way before paying attention. That's why well-organized and focused charts can be quickly and deeply absorbed and remembered by the human brain.

People often describe the visualizations as "charts" and "graphs." We may choose a term according to academic practice, or because we think it's important to distinguish the two terms, we can choose one of them. These two terms are used interchangeably and sometimes as synonyms. Sometimes people use these two terms to distinguish small differences between types of visualizations.

Typically, a chart is a graphic representation of data in a graph, diagram, map, or tabular form. You can imagine the most familiar charts, such as scatter charts, bar charts, line graphs, and pie charts. These chart types, or a combination of them, provide answers to most questions about relational data. These charts play a pivotal role in performing visual analysis of data.

Data visualization using charts relies on points drawn using Cartesian coordinate systems (e.g., X, Y, Z) along with a series of dimensions and measures. Dimensions (e.g., category, date, etc.) group measures to be analyzed. Then, we can create a visualization by rendering the measure to its coordinates. Some visualizations Excel at displaying many dimensions (such as an ordered bar chart), while others can support only a few dimensions (such as pie charts).

Each chart type has its pros and cons, but people will understand your data better with good use. If you focus on aesthetic conventions, you can also make your visualization beautiful. Use a combination of form and function to influence the way viewers perceive your data.

TABLEAU CATEGORIZING FIELDS

Some of the essential functions in Tableau will be frequently used in this book. Before jumping into the chart, we will describe Tableau's categorizing fields. More detailed information can also be found on Tableau's website[1].

- **Measures:** The quantitative values and can be aggregated. For example, sum, average, median, count, minimum, maximum, percentile, standard deviation, and variance values are the aggregated Measures. When dragging the measure to the worksheet, the data is automatically aggregated as a sum as a default setup.
- **Dimensions:** The qualitative values and can be used to describe the data with more details. For example, product names and production dates can be considered as Dimensions. They are typically used to categorize the data.
- **Discrete:** The values are distinct and separate from each other. It can be both Measures and Dimensions. It is shown as a blue pill in Tableau. For example, the defect event of a product (Yes or No) or the color of the product (blue and red) can be Discrete.
- **Continuous:** The values are not distinct and can be divided into smaller fractional and decimal values. It can be both Measures and Dimensions. It is shown as a green pill in Tableau. For example, the weight, height, width, and length can be Continuous.

2.1 STACKED BAR CHART

2.1.1 INTRODUCTION OF STACKED BAR CHART

A stacked bar chart is a type of vertical bar chart that consists of several categories. By seeing the portion of each divided segment, we can understand each category's relationship or part to the total amount of values. Table 2.1. shows the sample data set of ramen ratings (https://www.kaggle.com/residentmario/ramen-ratings). Our goal is to understand the critical factors affecting high ramen ratings. This information would be useful to improve the business to meet customers' satisfaction. We will use Tableau to conduct a quality analysis and step-by-step instructions will be provided.

TABLE 2.1
Sample Data Set of Ramen Ratings

Review number	Brand	Variety	Style	Country	Stars
2580	New Touch	T's Restaurant Tantanmen	Cup	Japan	3.75
2579	Just Way	Noodles Spicy Hot Sesame Spicy Hot Sesame Guan-Miao Noodles	Pack	Taiwan	1
2578	Nissin	Cup Noodles Chicken Vegetable	Cup	USA	2.25
2577	Wei Lih	GGE Ramen Snack Tomato Flavor	Pack	Taiwan	2.75
2576	Ching's Secret	Singapore Curry	Pack	India	3.75
2575	Samyang Foods	Kimchi song Song Ramen	Pack	South Korea	4.75
2574	Acecook	Spice Deli Tantan Men With Cilantro	Cup	Japan	4
2573	Ikeda Shoku	Nabeyaki Kitsune Udon	Tray	Japan	3.75
2572	Ripe'n'Dry	Hokkaido Soy Sauce Ramen	Pack	Japan	0.25
2571	KOKA	The Original Spicy Stir-Fried Noodles	Pack	Singapore	2.5
2570	Tao Kae Noi	Creamy Tom Yum Kung Flavour	Pack	Thailand	5
2569	Yamachan	Yokohama Tonkotsu Shoyu	Pack	USA	5
2568	Nongshim	Mr. Bibim Stir-Fried Kimchi Flavor	Pack	South Korea	4.25
2567	Nissin	Deka Buto Kimchi Pork Flavor	Bowl	Japan	4.5
2566	Nissin	Demae Ramen Bar Noodle Aka Tonkotsu Flavour Instant Noodle	Pack	Hong Kong	5

2.1.2 TABLEAU EXAMPLE

Step 1: Open Tableau. You may see this default screen (Figure 2.1).

Step 2: Drag the Excel data file onto Tableau, which will automatically open the Excel file (Figure 2.2).

Step 3: You may find the orange "Sheet1" at the bottom. Simple click this sheet. It will lead you to the worksheet (Figure 2.3).

Step 4: Now, you are on the worksheet. Several measures from the Excel file are shown in the left-hand-side panel. If we are interested in seeing ramen ratings, Drag the "Stars" variable into the Rows section [1] on the shelf. The Sum(Stars) will be shown as a default setting (Figure 2.4).

Step 5: If we are more interested in average values of ramen rating, right-click on the "Sum(Stars)" pill [1], and move to "Measure(Sum)" [2] then choose "Average" [3] (Figure 2.5).

Step 6: If we want to see ramen ratings by different countries, we can drag the "County" variable onto Columns on the shelf [1]. You may see the vertical bar chart of ramen ratings by multiple countries (Figure 2.6).

Step 7: Since there are too many countries shown in the plot, we may need to filter the top 5 countries that show high ramen ratings. Right-click on the "Country" pill [1], and select "Filter [2]" (Figure 2.7).

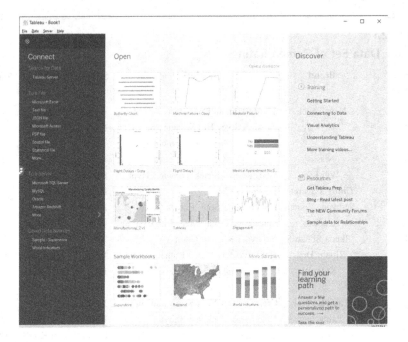

FIGURE 2.1   Step 1 in Section 2.1.

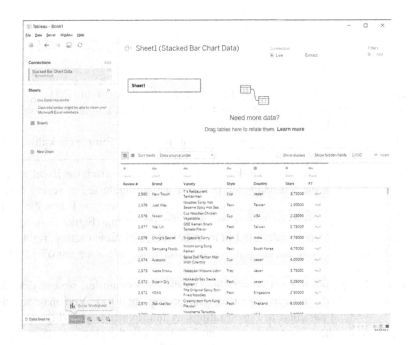

FIGURE 2.2   Step 2 in Section 2.1.

FIGURE 2.3   Step 3 in Section 2.1.

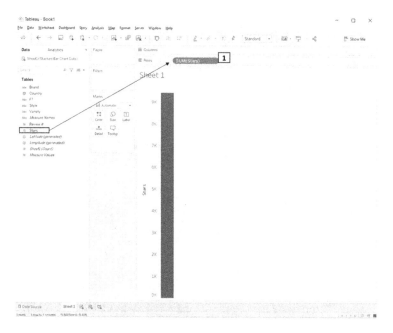

FIGURE 2.4   Step 4 in Section 2.1.

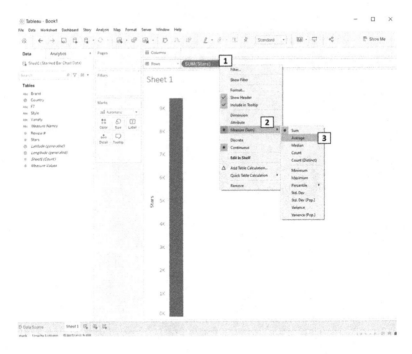

FIGURE 2.5 Step 5 in Section 2.1.

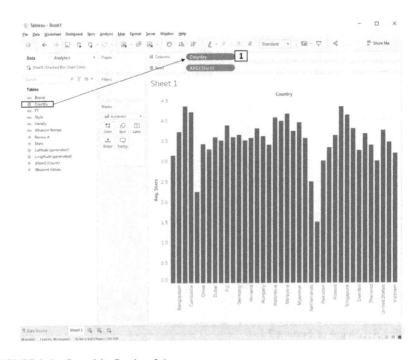

FIGURE 2.6 Step 6 in Section 2.1.

FIGURE 2.7 Step 7 in Section 2.1.

Step 8: You may see the pop-up box. Select the "Top" tab [1]. Check "By field" [2] and type 5 [3] to filter the top 5 countries that show high ramen ratings. Hit OK (Figure 2.8).

Step 9: Now, you would be able to see the top 5 countries (Figure 2.9).

Step 10: If we are interested in seeing the relationship between the Ramen style and ratings, drag "Style" onto "Color" under Marks [1]. You would see the stacked bar chart with different colors (Figure 2.10).

Step 11: If you want to see actual rating values by each style, press Ctrl and drag the "AVG(Stars)" pill to "Label" [1] under Marks. You would be able to see rating values per ramen style (Figure 2.11).

Step 12: If we want to fit stacked bar charts to the entire canvas, select "Entire View" on the toolbar (Figure 2.12).

Now, the final stacked bar chart was created. Different countries varied the preference of ramen style (Figure 2.13). For example, cup ramen showed the lowest ratings in Malaysia and Singapore, while Brazil showed the opposite trend. Box ramen style only existed in Malaysia, and it showed the highest rating. Both Sarawak and Cambodia only had one style (Pack) of ramen. There was no consistent trend in the relationship between ramen style and rating over different

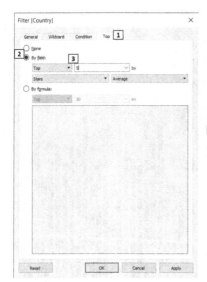

FIGURE 2.8   Step 8 in Section 2.1.

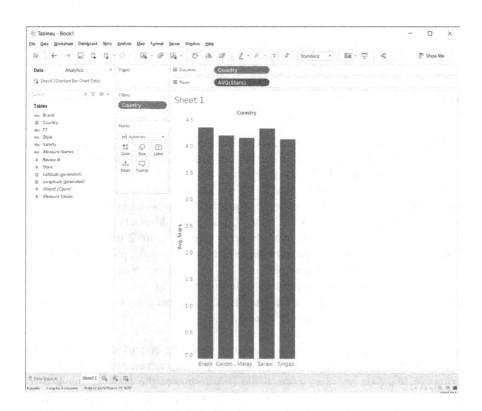

FIGURE 2.9   Step 9 in Section 2.1.

FIGURE 2.10 Step 10 in Section 2.1.

FIGURE 2.11 Step 11 in Section 2.1.

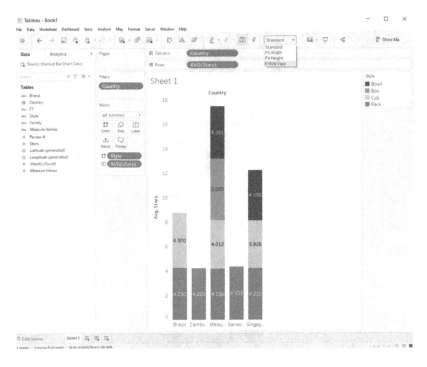

FIGURE 2.12   Step 12 in Section 2.1.

FIGURE 2.13   The final stacked bar chart of ramen ratings.

countries. More investigation would need a better understanding of critical factors affecting the ramen ratings.

2.2   HISTOGRAM

2.2.1   INTRODUCTION OF HISTOGRAM

The histogram is very commonly used in statistics. It is a graphical representation of the frequency distribution. To understand the histogram, we could study the frequency distribution first.

The frequency distribution is an efficient way to summarize the extensive data set into one table. This table consists of groups (i.e., classes) of the data, and the number of data values (i.e., frequencies) that belong to each group. For example, we have daily information about the number of defective items in a manufacturing plant. Table 2.2 shows the information about the data collected over ten days.

We could construct a frequency distribution table based on this raw data, as seen in Table 2.3. Each group (class) represents the number of defective items: {0, 1, 2, 3, 4}. The frequency represents the number of occurrences regarding each defective item group. After constructing a frequency distribution table, we could interpret that one defective item per day was the most common (frequency = 3) event. On the other hand, four defective items per day were the least common (frequency = 1) event in a manufacturing plant.

TABLE 2.2

Number of Defective Items Per Day Found in a Manufacturing Plant

Day 1	Day 2	Day 3	Day 4	Day 5	Day 6	Day 7	Day 8	Day 9	Day 10
0	1	2	3	4	0	1	2	1	3

TABLE 2.3

Frequency Distribution of the Number of Defective Items in a Manufacturing Plant

Defective	Frequency	Relative Frequency	Cumulative Frequency
0	2	0.2	2
1	3	0.3	5
2	2	0.2	7
3	2	0.2	9
4	1	0.1	10
Total Sum	10	1	

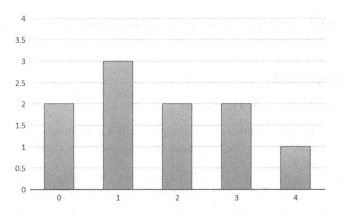

FIGURE 2.14   Histogram of the number of defective items in a manufacturing plant.

There are two different ways to assess the frequency distribution: relative and cumulative frequencies. The relative frequency is a proportion (%) of the data set that belongs to each group. Thus, the sum of relative frequencies should be one. The table shows the relative frequency of the number of defective items in a manufacturing plant. The equation is:

$$Relative \ frequency = \frac{Group \ (class) \ frequency}{\Sigma frequency} \qquad (2.1)$$

The cumulative frequency is the total frequency up to a given data value or group. The last value is always equal to the total sum of frequencies. The table shows the cumulative frequency of the number of defective items in a manufacturing plant.

If we transition from this tabular form of the frequency distribution to bar chart type, we could call it a histogram. The histogram is a special type of bar chart. Figure 2.14 shows the histogram regarding the number of defective items in a manufacturing plant. We could reach the same conclusion from the frequency distribution table. Since the histogram is visual and intuitive, it helps identify the frequency distribution pattern quickly. The next section will discuss how to utilize Tableau to construct the histograms.

2.2.2   TABLEAU EXAMPLE

Hospital wait times are known as one of the most significant factors affecting patient satisfaction. It is known that patients' processing time is tended to be greater than actual interaction time with a physician. The quality manager in the hospital wants to understand the pattern of hospital wait times. The hospital wait times (minutes) of 100 patients were randomly collected as sample data. Table 2.4 shows the hospital wait times (minutes) of 100 patients. Perform the following steps to construct the histogram using Tableau.

TABLE 2.4
Hospital Wait Times (Minutes) of 100 Patients

33	15	17	25	10	35	46	53	27	43
29	15	13	34	24	24	32	45	32	65
15	50	48	32	18	54	32	45	32	46
32	45	65	35	53	47	23	55	27	26
39	3	46	57	1	40	44	43	27	5
4	21	41	20	30	20	9	32	48	37
43	32	35	30	25	49	25	53	35	37
40	22	13	31	35	30	41	45	3	56
39	11	52	20	25	38	54	38	46	41
59	35	37	36	33	13	46	36	27	49

Step 1: Open Tableau and click on "Microsoft Excel." Upload the Excel file which contains the data or drag the data file onto the screen to upload it.

Step 2: Once the data file is uploaded, the data is adjusted into columns as shown in Figure 2.15. Then click on "sheet 1" at the bottom.

Step 3: Drag the "Hospital Wait Times (Minutes)" to the Columns shelf (Figure 2.16).

Step 4: Click "Show Me" on the toolbar. Select the histogram chart type (Figure 2.17).

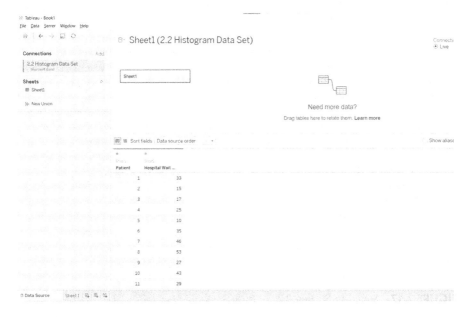

FIGURE 2.15 Step 2 in Section 2.2.

FIGURE 2.16 Step 3 in Section 2.2.

FIGURE 2.17 Step 4 in Section 2.2.

Step 5: On the "Hospital Wait Times (Minutes)(bin)," select "Edit" (Figure 2.18).
Step 6: Change the size of bins to "7" to have ten bins (Figure 2.19).
Step 7: Drag "(Hospital Wait Times (Minutes)" to "Color" Mark (Figure 2.20).
Step 8: Drag "Sheet1(Count): onto the "Label" Mark (Figure 2.21).
Step 9: Final histogram will be shown (Figure 2.22).

Based on the histogram, the patient's waiting time is commonly ranged between 35 and 42.5 minutes. More than 80% of patient waiting times occur between 20 and 55 minutes. In other words, patient waiting times of less than 15 minutes or more than 55 minutes are rare. Since patient waiting time is directly related to satisfaction, improvement methods to reduce waiting time will be essential.

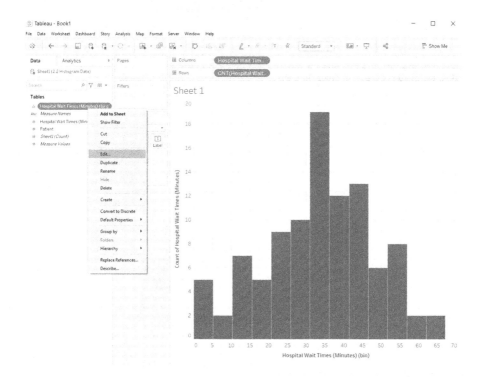

FIGURE 2.18   Step 5 in Section 2.2.

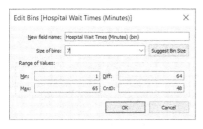

FIGURE 2.19   Step 6 in Section 2.2.

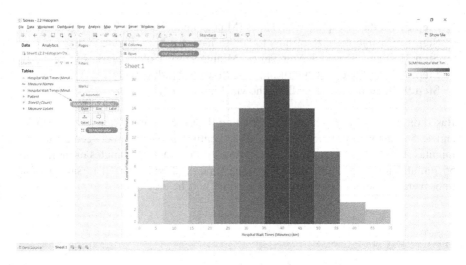

FIGURE 2.20   Step 7 in Section 2.2.

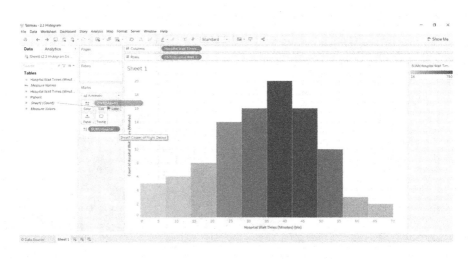

FIGURE 2.21   Step 8 in Section 2.2.

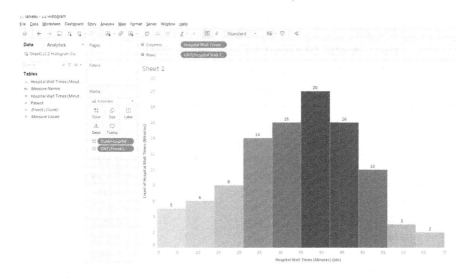

FIGURE 2.22   Final histogram.

2.3   BUTTERFLY CHART

2.3.1   INTRODUCTION OF BUTTERFLY CHART

The butterfly chart is useful to compare two data sets. It is often called the Tornado chart or Divergent chart. This chart uses horizontal bars for two data sets, and their X-axis values start from the center, which makes the plot like the butterfly wings.

2.3.2   TABLEAU EXAMPLE

Table 2.5 shows the flow width (microns) measurements data for two different Wafers types over ten days. The goal is to see any difference in flow width between two wafers over ten days.

> **Step 1:** Open the "Butterfly chart data" Excel file in Tableau. Click "Sheet1". You may be able to see the measure names in the left-hand side panel (Figure 2.23).
>
> **Step 2:** Drag and drop the "Day" in Rows [1] on the shelf. Drag and drop the "Wafer A" [2] and "Wafer B" [3] variables in the Columns in the shelf (Figure 2.24).
>
> **Step 3:** For the drop-down menu [1] in Marks, select the "Bar" shape [2] (Figure 2.25).
>
> **Step 4:** Right-click a blank space on the left sidebar and choose "Create calculated field" (Figure 2.26).
>
> **Step 5:** Create "Central Axis" and set 0 value. Hit OK (Figure 2.27).

TABLE 2.5

Flow Width (Microns) Measurement Data for Two Different Wafers Over 10 Days

Day	Wafer A	Wafer B
1	1.597	1.4128
2	1.6887	1.3592
3	1.4720	1.4039
4	1.1449	1.5821
5	1.3688	1.4738
6	1.5220	1.3281
7	1.7559	1.4177
8	1.1928	1.5265
9	1.6914	1.3574
10	1.4573	1.5089

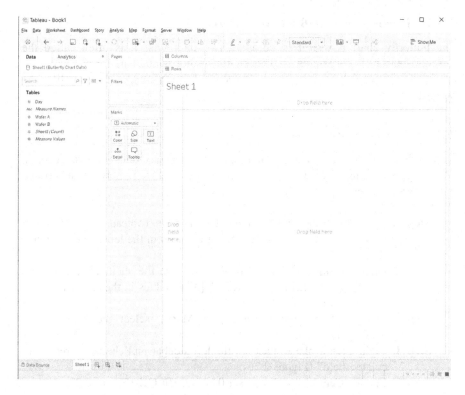

FIGURE 2.23 Step 1 in Section 2.3.

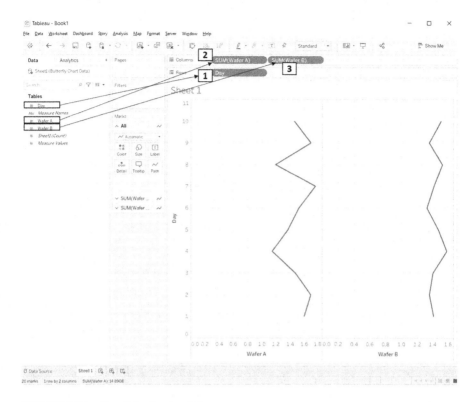

FIGURE 2.24 Step 2 in Section 2.3.

FIGURE 2.25 Step 3 in Section 2.3.

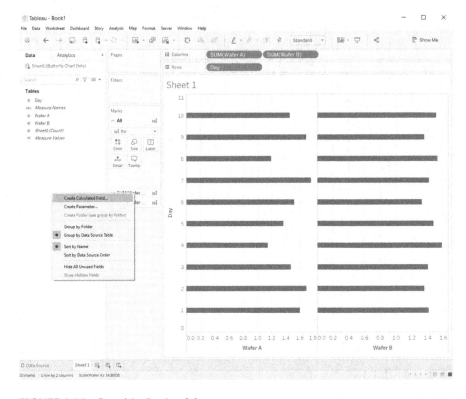

FIGURE 2.26   Step 4 in Section 2.3.

FIGURE 2.27   Step 5 in Section 2.3.

Step 6: Drag and drop the "Central Axis" between the "Wafer A" and "Wafer B" pills [1] in the Columns (Figure 2.28).

Step 7: Select the Central Axis section in Marks [1]. Drag and drop "Day" in Label under Marks [2]. Select "Text" shape [3] for the drop-down menu under Marks (Figure 2.29).

Step 8: Right-click around "Central Axis" and select "Edit Axis" (Figure 2.30).

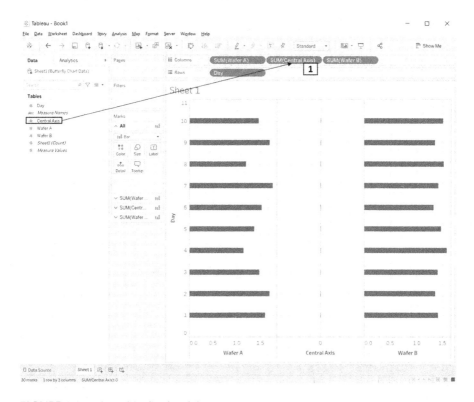

FIGURE 2.28 Step 6 in Section 2.3.

FIGURE 2.29 Step 7 in Section 2.3.

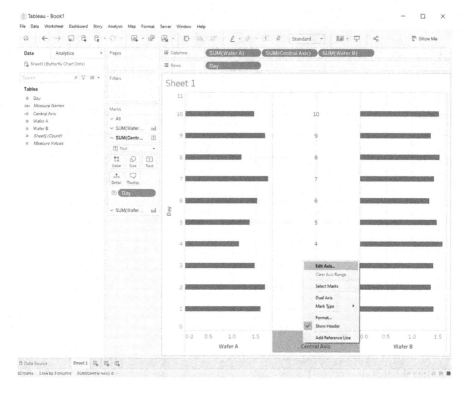

FIGURE 2.30   Step 8 in Section 2.3.

Step 9: Go to the Tick Marks tab and set both Major and Minor tick marks as none (Figure 2.31).

Step 10: Right-click around "Day" and uncheck "Show Header" for Wafer A (Figure 2.32).

Step 11: Right-click around "Wafer A" and select "Edit Axis" (Figure 2.33).

Step 12: Under the General tab, check the scale as "Reversed" (Figure 2.34).

Step 13: Under the SUM(Central Axis) pill, right-click and select "Dual Axis" (Figure 2.35).

Step 14: Right-click around "Wafer A" then check "Synchronize Axis" of Wafer A (Figure 2.36).

Step 15: Right-click around "Wafer A" and select "Edit Axis" for "Wafer A" variable. Under the General tab, set 0 as a Fixed start and set Automatic as an end (Figure 2.37).

Step 16: Similarly, drag and drop "Central Axis" in the Columns right next to "SUM (Wafer B)" pill [1]. Drag and drop "Day" variable Label for SUM (Central Axis) under Marks [2]. Select "Text" [3] for the drop-down menu (Figure 2.38).

Step 17: Right-click around "Central Axis" then check "Dual Axis" for the Central Axis (Figure 2.39).

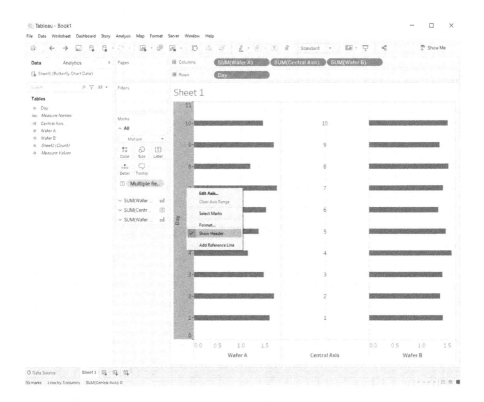

FIGURE 2.31   Step 9 in Section 2.3.

FIGURE 2.32   Step 10 in Section 2.3.

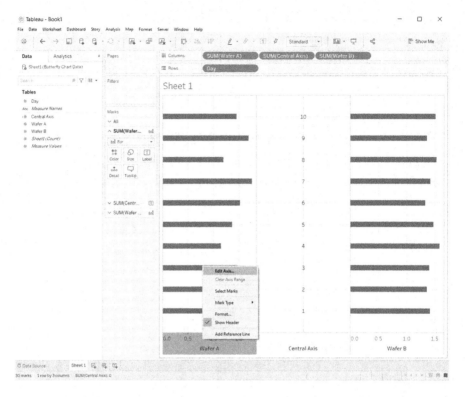

FIGURE 2.33   Step 11 in Section 2.3.

FIGURE 2.34   Step 12 in Section 2.3.

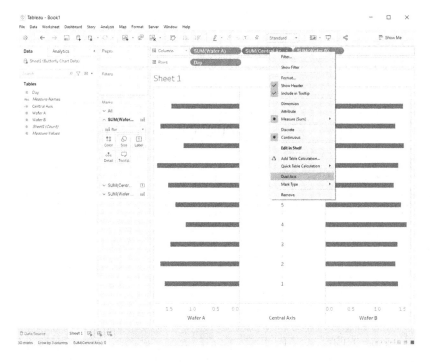

FIGURE 2.35 Step 13 in Section 2.3.

FIGURE 2.36 Step 14 in Section 2.3.

FIGURE 2.37   Step 15 in Section 2.3.

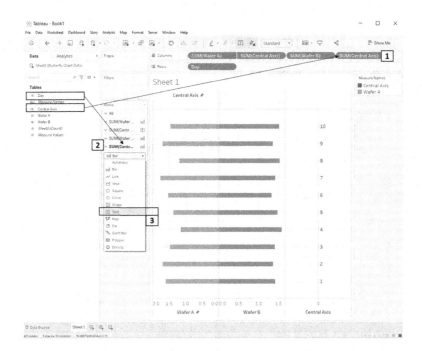

FIGURE 2.38   Step 16 in Section 2.3.

Step 18: Right-click around "Wafer B" then check "Synchronize Axis" of "Wafer B" variable (Figure 2.40).

Step 19: Right-click around "Wafer B" then select "Edit Axis" of the "Wafer B" variable. Set "Fixed start" as 0 and "Fixed end" as 2 (Figure 2.41).

FIGURE 2.39 Step 17 in Section 2.3.

FIGURE 2.40 Step 18 in Section 2.3.

FIGURE 2.41   Step 19 in Section 2.3.

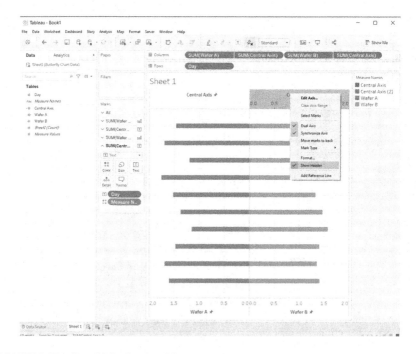

FIGURE 2.42   Step 20 in Section 2.3.

Step 20: Right-click then uncheck "Show Header" of "Wafer B" variable (Figure 2.42).

You would be able to see the final butterfly chart.

FIGURE 2.43 The final butterfly chart of the flow width in Wafers A and B.

Based on the butterfly chart (Figure 2.43), we can see that Wafer A tends to have a larger flow width than Wafer B. In addition, Wafer A has more variation of the flow width over ten days compared to Wafer B. It suggests that Wafer B may have a better quality control of the flow width than Wafer A.

2.4 DONUT CHART

2.4.1 INTRODUCTION OF DONUT CHART

Donut charts are a type of pie chart that shows the proportion of categorical data. The proportion of individual categories is related to the size of each piece in the chart. On top of that, there is a hole in the middle, which differentiates from a traditional pie chart. The information of the total amount of data often is shown in this hole. Table 2.6 shows the sample data of video game sales (https://www. kaggle.com/gregorut/videogamesales), consisting of rank, genre, publisher, and global sales amount (in millions) worldwide. There 16,598 records of the information in the full data set. We could use Tableau to understand which genre accounts high portion of global sales in a video game. This would help understand the potential needs of the video game that will be published by the company.

TABLE 2.6
The Sample Data Set of Video Game Sales

Rank	Genre	Publisher	Global Sales
1	Sports	Nintendo	82.74
2	Platform	Nintendo	40.24
3	Racing	Nintendo	35.82
4	Sports	Nintendo	33
5	Role-Playing	Nintendo	31.37
6	Puzzle	Nintendo	30.26
7	Platform	Nintendo	30.01
8	Misc	Nintendo	29.02
9	Platform	Nintendo	28.62
10	Shooter	Nintendo	28.31
11	Simulation	Nintendo	24.76
12	Racing	Nintendo	23.42
13	Role-Playing	Nintendo	23.1
14	Sports	Nintendo	22.72
15	Sports	Nintendo	22

2.4.2 TABLEAU EXAMPLE

Step 1: Open Tableau and drag the data source Excel file onto Tableau.

Step 2: Click "Sheet1" to go to Worksheet.

Step 3: Select "Pie" shape under Marks [1] (Figure 2.44).

Step 4: Drag and drop "Genre" in Color under Marks [1]. Drag and drop "Genre" in Label under Marks as well [2]. Drag and drop "Global Sales" in Angle under Marks [3]. Change the view from "Standard" to "Entire View" [4] (Figure 2.45).

Step 5: Place the cursor on the blank space below the "measure values" on the screen's left side and right-click of "Create Calculated Field" then create a calculated field of 1, which will align different charts later (Figure 2.46).

Step 6: Drag and drop "1" in the Rows [1]. Click [2] and Set Measure (Minimum) [3] (Figure 2.47).

Step 7: Press Ctrl and drag and drop "Min(1)" fill to the right [1] (Figure 2.48).

Step 8: Set the shape as "Circle" under MIN(1)(2) Marks. Remove all pills under the Marks [1] (Figure 2.49).

Step 9: Drag and drop "Global Sales" to Label under Marks [1]. Click Label [2] then select and change the Label Alignment to center [3] (Figure 2.50).

Step 10: Change the Colors to white [1]. Click the second MIN(1) under

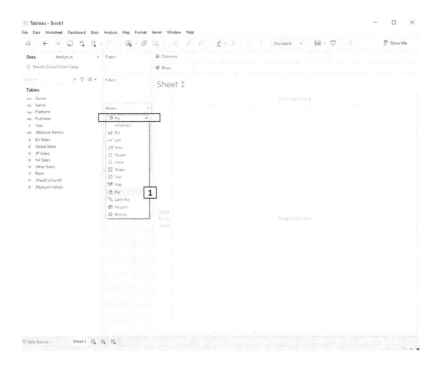

FIGURE 2.44   Step 3 in Section 2.4.

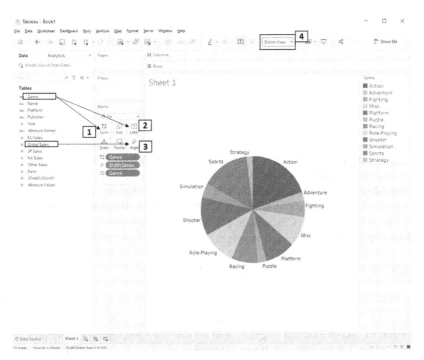

FIGURE 2.45   Step 4 in Section 2.4.

FIGURE 2.46   Step 5 in Section 2.4.

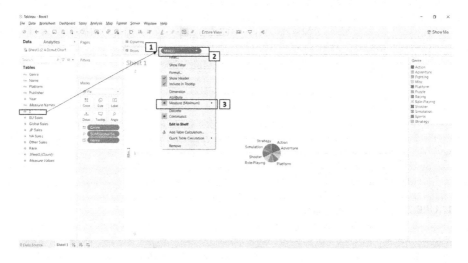

FIGURE 2.47   Step 6 in Section 2.4.

Rows [2] and set the "Dual Axis" for the second MIN(1) pill [3] (Figure 2.51).

Step 11: Click the Min(1) [1] under Marks then change the Size [2] to change the pie chart's size then follow the same steps for the Min(1)(2) to get the shape of a donut (Figure 2.52).

Step 12: Drag and drop "Global Sales" in Label of the pie chart (MIN(1)) [1]. Click SUM(Global Sales) [2] then select "Percent of Total" under Quick Table Calculation [3] (Figure 2.53).

Step 13: Right-Click around the right axis and unselect "Show Header" on the axis (Figure 2.54).

Step 14: Final donut chart was made (Figure 2.55).

The action genre showed the highest proportion of global sales, followed by Sports based on the donut chart. On the other hand, the Strategy genre showed the lowest proportion of global sales. It suggests that action and sports genres generally have greater demands than different types of genres.

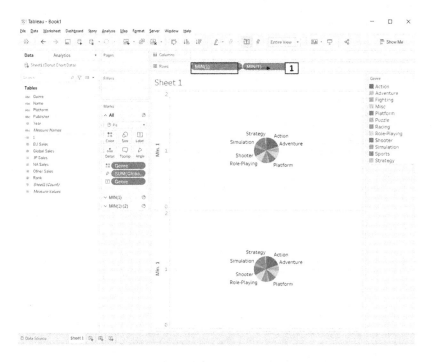

FIGURE 2.48 Step 7 in Section 2.4.

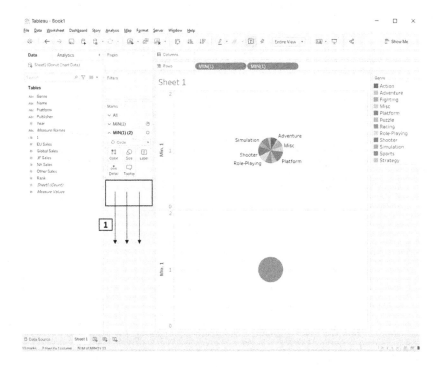

FIGURE 2.49 Step 8 in Section 2.4.

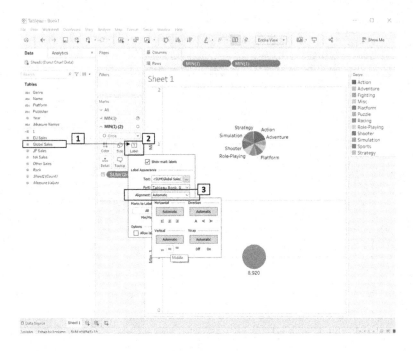

FIGURE 2.50 Step 9 in Section 2.4.

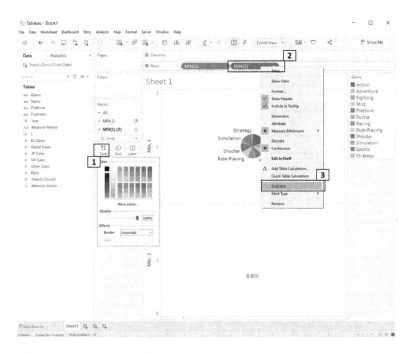

FIGURE 2.51 Step 10 in Section 2.4.

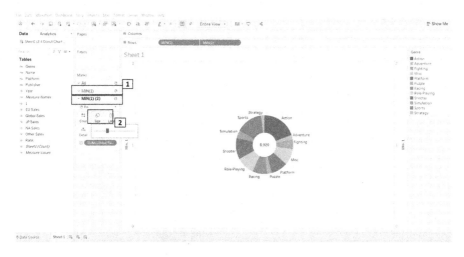

FIGURE 2.52   Step 11 in Section 2.4.

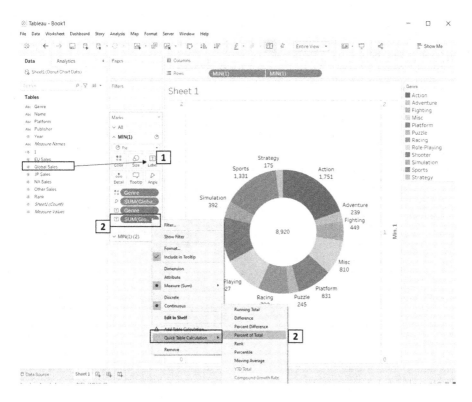

FIGURE 2.53   Step 12 in Section 2.4.

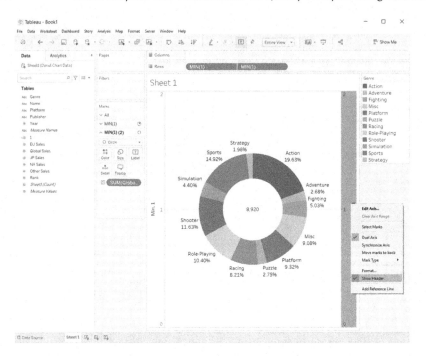

FIGURE 2.54 Step 13 in Section 2.4.

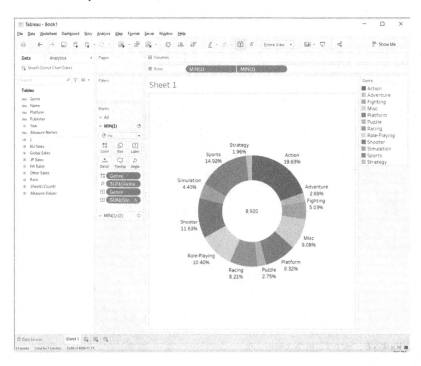

FIGURE 2.55 Final donut chart.

2.5   SCATTER PLOT

2.5.1   INTRODUCTION OF SCATTER PLOT

The scatter plot helps to understand the relationship between two variables. Each symbol (e.g., dot) in the graph represents a data pair. For example, we are interested in finding the relationship between the average daily temperate (°C) and the number of beach visitors. It is essential to determine if the number of beach visitors (dependent variable) depends on the average daily temperature (independent variable). Table 2.7 shows the sample data of these variables over 12 days.

For constructing the scatter plot, we could assign an independent variable (e.g., average daily temperature) at X-axis, and a dependent variable (e.g., number of beach visitors) at Y-axis, as seen in Figure 2.56. Each data point is located at the intersection of two variables, which represent the data pair. Based on the visualization of the scatter plot, we could recognize the strong relationship between the two variables. The trend line could be added to visualize their relationship better. In this example, the linear trendline fits the data points well. As the average daily temperature goes up, the number of beach visitors is also tended to increase. The next section will describe the use of Tableau to construct the scatter plot.

2.5.2   TABLEAU EXAMPLE

The fuel economy (MPG: miles per gallon) of cars is an important factor for numerous commuters and business stakeholders. This fuel economy may be related to the car mass itself. Heavier vehicles could consume more fuel than lighter vehicles. Table 2.8 describes the city MPG, high MPG, and car mass of

---

TABLE 2.7

The Sample Data of the Average Daily Temperature and the Number of Beach Visitors over 12 Days

Average Daily Temperature (°C)	Number of Beach Visitors
24	230
26	335
22	190
25	332
29	410
32	530
29	420
35	614
33	560
28	440
33	460
27	350

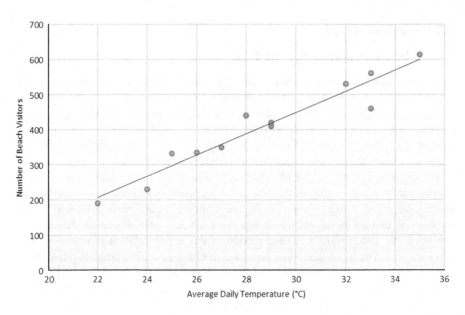

FIGURE 2.56   Scatter plot of the average daily temperature and the number of beach visitors.

TABLE 2.8
City and Highway MPG and Car Mass (kg) of 20 Random Cars

City MPG	Highway MPG	Car Mass (kg)
11	17	1695
13	19	1548
12	19	1548
12	19	1560
21	29	1146
14	23	1726
16	26	1519
9	14	1650
13	21	1912
11	18	2018
12	19	2007
19	27	1305
19	27	1330
16	25	1663
25	33	1209
19	26	1483
17	26	1610
25	34	1155
22	30	1276
16	24	1520

20 random cars (adapted from https://www.wired.com/2012/08/fuel-economy-vs-mass/). If there is a strong relationship, this could be a good justification to reduce the cars' weight to improve MPG. Perform the following steps to construct the scatter chart using Tableau.

The data structure could be modified to construct the scatter plot efficiently using Tableau, as seen in Table 2.9. This only shows the partial data due to the data size.

Step 1: Open Tableau and click on "Microsoft Excel." Upload the Excel file which contains the data or drag the data file onto the screen to upload it.

Step 2: Once the data file is uploaded, the data is adjusted into columns as shown in Figure 2.57. Then click on "sheet 1" at the bottom.

Step 3: Drag the "Car Mass(kg)" measure to the Columns shelf [1] and "MPG" measure to the Rows shelf [2]. Click "Show Me" on the toolbar. Select the Scatter Plot chart type. Then drag "Label" dimension to "Color" in the Marks [3] as seen in Figure 2.58.

Step 4: Since the data is aggregated, click on "analysis" and unselect "aggregate measures" as seen in Figure 2.59.

Step 5: To adjust the range of data in the X axis, right-click in the X-axis area [1], then select "Edit Axis." In the pop-up (Edit Axis [Car Mass(kg)], uncheck the box for "Include zero" [2] (Figure 2.60).

Step 6: In the section "Analytics," drag the Trend line to charts and select "Linear," as shown in Figure 2.61. Then can see the trend line in the Scatter Plot, as shown in Figure 2.62.

Step 7: Final scatter plot is shown.

TABLE 2.9

The Data Structure of the City and Highway MPG and Car Mass (kg)

MPG	Label	Car Mass (kg)
11	City	1695
13	City	1548
12	City	1548
12	City	1560
21	City	1146
17	Highway	1695
19	Highway	1548
19	Highway	1548
19	Highway	1560
29	Highway	1146

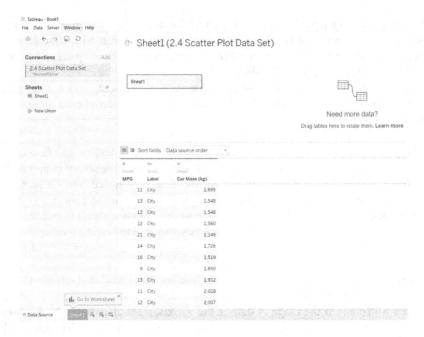

FIGURE 2.57   Step 2 in Section 2.5.

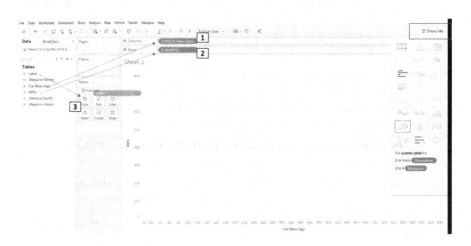

FIGURE 2.58   Step 3 in Section 2.5.

As we can see from the scatter plot, as the car's mass increases, the MPG tends to decrease. Whether driving on the highway or driving in the city, this trend is similar, which can be seen from a similar linear trend line slope. From a manufacturer's point of view, it would be more advantageous in terms of fuel efficiency to develop a car that weighs less compared to its competitors producing comparable

FIGURE 2.59 Step 4 in Section 2.5.

FIGURE 2.60 Step 5 in Section 2.5.

vehicles. From the driver's point of view, avoiding unnecessary loading items into the car as much as possible would be a good way to increase fuel efficiency.

FIGURE 2.61   Step 6 in Section 2.5.

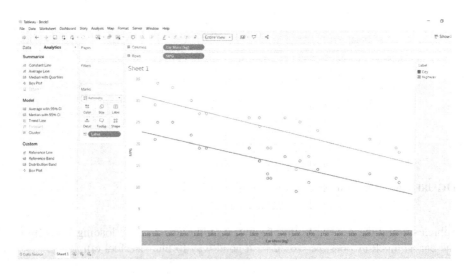

FIGURE 2.62   Final scatter plot.

2.6   BUBBLE CHART

2.6.1   INTRODUCTION OF BUBBLE CHART

The bubble chart is useful to describe the information of three different variables. Two variables information can be located on the x-axis and y-axis on the plot, similar to the scatter plot. The size of the bubble can depict the last variable. Based on the bubble size visualization, it is easy to understand the relative differences across different conditions. Thus, the bubble chart allows us to understand the three-way relationship between measures. Table 2.10 shows Starbucks sales, including revenue and net income and the number of employees from 2005 to 2019.

The bubble chart helps understand the relationship between these three measures, as seen in Figure 2.63. Revenue data is located on the x-axis, and net income data is placed on the y-axis. The size of bubbles indicates the number of employees. As expected, there is a strong relationship between revenue and net income. As the revenue grows, the net income is tended to increase as well. This relationship is also aligned with the employees. As both the revenue and net income growth, the number of employees tends to expand. The next section will describe the ways to construct the bubble chart using Tableau.

2.6.2   TABLEAU EXAMPLE

Table 2.11 describes the graduation admission data, including GRE score, letter of recommendation strength (LOR), research experience, and admission chance. This

TABLE 2.10
Starbucks Sales and Employees Data

Year	Revenue in mil. US$	Net Income in mil. US$	Employees
2005	6,369	494	115,000
2006	7,787	564	145,800
2007	9,412	673	172,000
2008	10,383	316	176,000
2009	9,775	391	142,000
2010	10,707	946	137,000
2011	11,700	1,246	149,000
2012	13,277	1,384	160,000
2013	14,867	8	182,000
2014	16,448	2,068	191,000
2015	19,163	2,757	238,000
2016	21,316	2,818	254,000
2017	22,387	2,885	277,000
2018	24,720	4,518	291,000
2019	26,509	3,599	346,000

(Adapted from https://en.wikipedia.org/wiki/Starbucks)

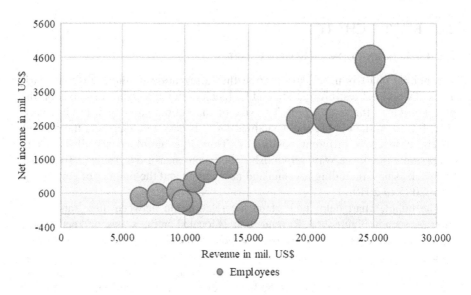

FIGURE 2.63   The bubble chart of Starbucks sales and employees (for years 2005 to 2019).

TABLE 2.11

Graduate Admission Data (Adapted from (Acharya, Armaan, & Antony, 2019))

Serial No.	GRE Score	LOR	Research Experience	Chance of Admit
1	337	4.5	Research	0.92
2	324	4.5	Research	0.76
3	316	3.5	Research	0.72
4	322	2.5	Research	0.8
5	314	3	No Research	0.65
6	330	3	Research	0.9
7	321	4	Research	0.75
8	308	4	No Research	0.68
9	302	1.5	No Research	0.5
10	323	3	No Research	0.45
11	325	4	Research	0.52
12	327	4.5	Research	0.84
13	328	4.5	Research	0.78
14	307	3	Research	0.62
15	311	2	Research	0.61
16	314	2.5	No Research	0.54
17	317	3	No Research	0.66
18	319	3	Research	0.65
19	318	3	No Research	0.63
20	303	3	No Research	0.62

Note: LOR = letter of recommendation strength.

information was randomly collected for 20 applicants. Understanding the relationship between variables would be helpful to predict graduate admission. Students could prioritize their effort to increase the chance of admission. Perform the following steps to construct the bubble chart using Tableau.

Step 1: Open Tableau and click on "Microsoft Excel." Upload the Excel file which contains the data or drag the data file onto the screen to upload it.

Step 2: Once the data file is uploaded, the data is adjusted into columns as shown in Figure 2.64. Then click on "sheet 1" at the bottom.

Step 3: Drag the "GRE Score" measure to the Columns shelf [1] and the "Chance of Admit" measure to the Rows shelf [2]. Then drag the "Research" dimension to "Color" [3] and drag the "LOR" measure to "Size" in the Marks as seen in Figure 2.65. For the drop-down menu under the "Marks," select the "Circle."

Step 4: Since the data is aggregated, click on "analysis" and unselect "aggregate measures" as seen in Figure 2.66.

Step 5: To adjust the range of data in the X-axis, right-click in the X-axis area, then select "Edit Axis." In the pop-up (Edit Axis [GRE Score]), uncheck the box for "Include zero" (Figure 2.67).

FIGURE 2.64 Step 2 in Section 2.6.

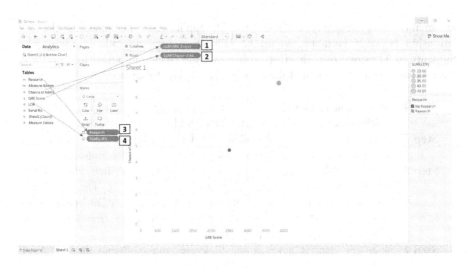

FIGURE 2.65 Step 3 in Section 2.6.

FIGURE 2.66 Step 4 in Section 2.6.

Step 6: To adjust the bubble's size and color opacity, click "Color" and "Size" in the Marks and change them as desired (Figure 2.68).

Step 7: Final bubble chart is shown in Figure 2.69.

As seen from the bubble chart, the higher the GRE score, the higher the admission chance. Also, students with research experience tended to have higher GRE scores

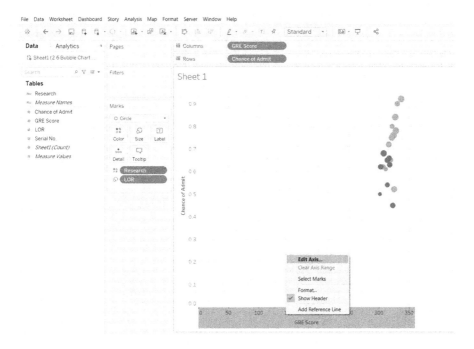

FIGURE 2.67 Step 5 in Section 2.6.

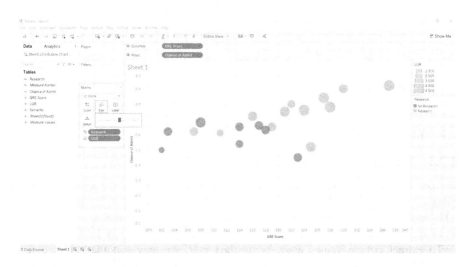

FIGURE 2.68 Step 6 in Section 2.6.

and a higher chance of admission than those who did not. It was found that the strength of the letter of recommendation was also significant in the group with high GRE scores and high admission chances. In sum, students with a high college acceptance rate show Excellent performance in various fields such as research, letters of recommendation, and GRE.

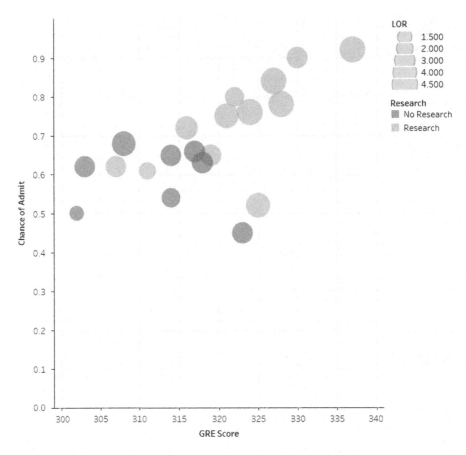

FIGURE 2.69   Final bubble chart.

2.7   BOX PLOT

2.7.1   Introduction of Box Plot

The box plot (or the box and whisker plot) is useful to understand the spread of data using five key numbers (minimum value, first quartile (Q1), median (Q2), third quartile (Q3), and maximum value). In some cases, the box plot also shows the outliers. Here is an example of the number of account errors over 12 days, as seen in Table 2.12.

To extract critical values used for the box plot, we may sort the values first. Table 2.13 shows the sorted values from the lowest value to the highest value. Based on this, we could first identify the median value (Q2) as 13, which is located between the 6th and 7th values. The first quartile (Q1) value can be identified as 12, which is located between the 3rd and 4th values. The third quartile (Q3) value is 14, which is the values between 9th and 10th. The minimum value is ten and the maximum value is 23. However, if outliers exist, these minimum or maximum values could be changed. To identify the outlier, the interquartile range (IQR) can be calculated by the third

TABLE 2.12

The Number of Accounting Errors Over 12 Days

Day 1	Day 2	Day 3	Day 4	Day 5	Day 6
13	14	10	11	14	17
Day 7	Day 8	Day 9	Day 10	Day 11	Day 12
23	12	14	12	12	13

TABLE 2.13

Sorted Values of the Number of Accounting Errors

Day	Number of Accounting Errors
3	10
4	11
8	12
11	12
10	12
1	13
12	13
2	14
9	14
5	14
6	17
7	23

quartile minus the first quartile, and the value is 2. The high value is computed using Equation 2.2, and the value is $14 + 1.5 \times 2 = 17$. The low value is calculated by the Equation 2.3, and the value is $11.5 - 1.5 \times 2 = 8.5$. If any values are below the low value (8.5) or above the high value (17), they can be identified as outliers. In this example, 23 account errors (Day 7) are beyond the high value, so it is an outlier. In this case, the maximum value can be changed from 23 to 17 (second highest value).

$$\text{High value} = Q3 + 1.5 \times IQR \tag{2.2}$$

$$\text{Low value} = Q1 - 1.5 \times IQR \tag{2.3}$$

Based on this key information, Figure 2.70 is the box plot of the number of accounting errors. The box shows the Q1 (12), median (13), and Q3 (14) values. Within the box, "X" represents the average value of the number of accounting errors (13.75). The other two vertical lines extending from the box are called

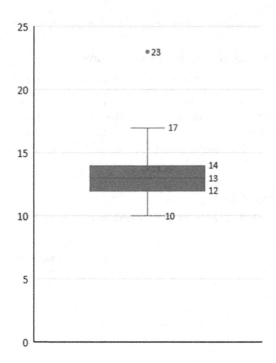

FIGURE 2.70   The box plot of the number of accounting errors.

"whiskers." The maximum value shows 17, and the minimum value shows 10. One data point is far beyond the maximum value, which is an outlier (23). Based on this box plot, we could identify that one extreme number of accounting errors occurred on day 7. In general, the number of accounting errors is tightly grouped and centered around the median value. This indicates that the number of accounting errors has low variability or dispersion. The next section will describe the step-by-step methods of using Tableau to construct the box plot.

2.7.2 TABLEAU EXAMPLE

This example shows the student performance in exams, including math, reading, and writing scores, as seen in Table 2.14. It is assumed that test preparation would increase the students' performance. The box plot would help understand the variability of each exam score with and without the test preparation course. Perform the following steps to construct the box plot using Tableau.

For the convenient use of Tableau, the data structure was modified as seen in Table 2.15, which only shows partial data as an example.

Step 1: Open Tableau and click on "Microsoft Excel". Upload the Excel file which contains the data or drag the data file onto the screen to upload it.

TABLE 2.14

Student Performance in Exams (Adapted from http://roycekimmons.com/ tools/generated_data/exams)

Test Preparation Course	Math Score	Reading Score	Writing Score
none	72	72	74
completed	69	90	88
none	90	95	93
none	47	57	44
none	76	78	75
none	71	83	78
completed	88	95	92
none	40	43	39
completed	64	64	67
none	38	60	50
none	58	54	52
none	40	52	43
none	65	81	73
completed	78	72	70
none	50	53	58
none	69	75	78
none	88	89	86
none	18	32	28
completed	46	42	46
none	54	58	61

TABLE 2.15

The Data Structure of Student Performance in Exams

Test Preparation Course	Score	Exam Type
none	72	Math
none	72	Reading
none	74	Writing
completed	69	Math
completed	90	Reading
completed	88	Writing

Step 2: Once the data file is uploaded, the data is adjusted into columns as shown in Figure 2.71. Then click on "sheet 1" at the bottom.

Step 3: Drag the "Test Preparation Course" and "Exam Type" to the Columns shelf [1][2] and "Score" measure to the Rows shelf [3] as seen in Figure 2.72.

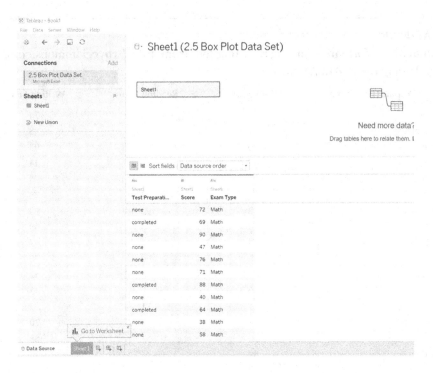

FIGURE 2.71   Step 2 in Section 2.7.

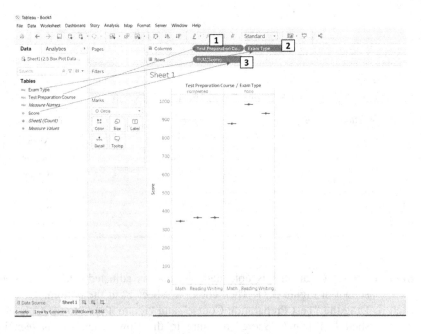

FIGURE 2.72   Step 3 in Section 2.7.

Step 4: Since the data is aggregated, click on "analysis" and unselect "aggregate measures" as seen in Figure 2.73 and make sure that the type of chart is Box Plot chart type in "Show Me" on the toolbar as seen in Figure 2.73.

Step 5: Drag "Exam Type" dimension to "Color" in the Marks to differentiate the color per each "Exam Type" as seen in Figure 2.74. To get the entire view of the Box Plot Chart, click on the "Standard" drop-down arrow, located on the top toolbar, and then select "Entire View."

Step 6: Final box plot is shown (Figure 2.75).

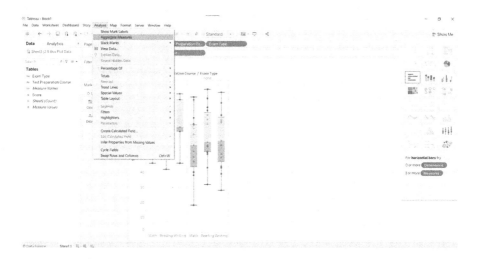

FIGURE 2.73 Step 4 in Section 2.7.

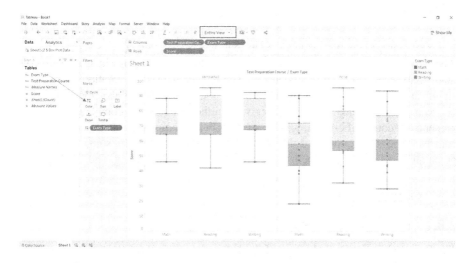

FIGURE 2.74 Step 5 in Section 2.7.

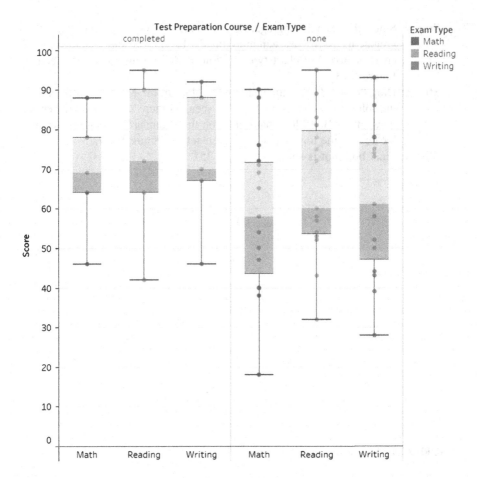

FIGURE 2.75   Final box plot.

If we look at the box plot, students who took test preparation courses scored higher than those who did not participate in math, reading, and writing. In particular, for mathematics, the variation of students who completed the test preparation course was significantly less than that of those who did not. This indicates that the difference between students' mathematics grades was further reduced by completing the test preparation course. For writing, the students who completed the test preparation courses were more clustered in scores above the median. In sum, taking test preparation courses greatly helps improve grades in math, reading, and writing.

2.8   PARETO CHART

2.8.1   INTRODUCTION OF PARETO CHART

The Pareto chart is a combination of the bar and the line chart. The chart is related to the 80-20 rule. This rule indicates that 80% of the problems are related to 20% of the reasons. For example, this Table 2.16 shows different defect types and the number of defects in the footwear.

If we construct the Pareto chart based on the table, we could sort the number of defects from the highest to the lowest value. Figure 2.76 shows the Pareto chart of the defects in the footwear. The horizontal x-axis indicates the categories (e.g., defect types). The "open seam" defect type shows the highest frequency (113 defects) and is followed by the "uneven stitches" defect type (11 defects). There are two y-axes in the Pareto chart. The left-hand side y-axis represents the frequency (e.g., number of defects), and the right-hand side y-axis indicates the percentage of events (e.g., defects). The bar chart is related to the number of defects for each defect type. The line chart shows the cumulative percentage of total defects. The "open seam" defect accounts for 80% of total defects, so this defect could have a higher priority for improvement than others. The improvement of this "open seam" defect would have the greatest impact on the process. This is aligned with the 80-20 rule. The "open seam" defect type only accounts for 20% of defect types (1/5). But these vital few defect types could account for 80% of the total number of defects. Thus, the Pareto chart helps determine which defects we should focus on the initial improvements to produce the most significant

---

TABLE 2.16

List of Different Defect Types and the Number of Defects in the Footwear

Defect Type	Open Seam	Wrinkle	Uneven stitches	Uncut Thread End	Loose Yarn
Count	113	5	11	10	3

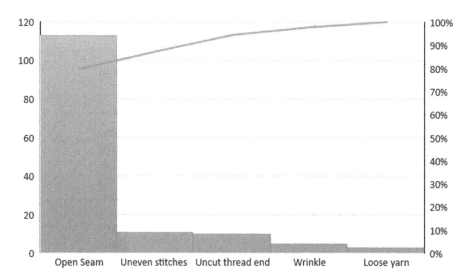

FIGURE 2.76 Pareto chart of the defects in the footwear.

impact. The next section will describe how to use Tableau to construct the Pareto chart.

2.8.2 Tableau Example

The flight delays are critically related to the customer's satisfaction and the business of air carriers. Increased travel time could result in the stress and fatigue of passengers. Airlines also struggle with extra costs dealing with the extra crew costs and accommodation fees of disrupted passengers. Several causes of flight delays have been reported. Table 2.17 shows the number of occurrences per cause of flight delays in a one-year period. The quality analyst wants to understand the primary causes affecting flight delays. This information would be helpful to improve logistics and airline service. Perform the following steps to construct the Pareto chart using Tableau.

Step 1: Open Tableau and click on "Microsoft Excel." Upload the Excel file which contains the data or drag the data file onto the screen to upload it.

Step 2: Once the data file is uploaded, the data is adjusted into columns as shown in Figure 2.77. Then click on "sheet 1" at the bottom.

Step 3: First, drag the "Causes of Flight Delays" dimension to the Columns shelf [1]. Second, drag the "count" to the rows shelf [2] as shown in Figure 2.78.

Step 4: Click the icon in the toolbar of "Sorted descending by the sum of Count within Causes of Flight Delays" [1] as shown in Figure 2.79.

Step 5: Press Ctrl and drag "SUM(Count)" pill to the right next to the pill [1] as shown in Figure 2.80.

TABLE 2.17
Cause of Flight Delays and Their Occurrences in One Year

Cause of Flight Delays	Count
Air Carrier Delay	225,000
Aircraft Arriving Late	287,500
Security Delay	5,000
National Aviation System Delay	132,500
Extreme Weather	15,000
Closed Runway	30,000
Earthquakes and tsunamis	5,000
Fueling	25,000
Terrorist Attacks	2,500
Other	10,000

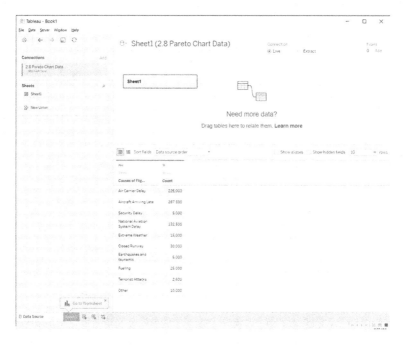

FIGURE 2.77 Step 2 in Section 2.8.

Step 6: Under the Marks of the second "SUM(Count)," [1] set "Line." [2] as shown in Figure 2.81.

Step 7: Right-click around the Axis ("Count") for the line chart [1] then select "Dual Axis" on the Y-axis of the line chart [2] as shown in Figure 2.82.

Step 8: On the second pill of "SUM(Count)," [1] select "Quick Table Calculation" [2] and "Running Total." [3] as shown in Figure 2.83.

Step 9: On the second pill of "SUM(Count)", [1] select "Edit Table Calculation" [2] as shown in Figure 2.84.

Step 10: Check "Add secondary calculation". Select "Percent of Total" in the secondary calculation type [1] as shown in Figure 2.85.

Step 11: Under the Color in Marks for the line chart (the second SUM(count) [1], change the line color [2] as shown in Figure 2.86.

Step 12: Right-click around the right-hand side Y-axis [1] then select "Add Reference Line" [2] as shown in Figure 2.87.

Step 13: Under "Line," select "Constant" and set "0.8" as shown in Figure 2.88.

Step 14: Final Pareto chart is shown in Figure 2.89.

Based on the Pareto chart, air carriers arriving late and air carrier delay accounted for more than 70% of the total flight delay issues. These two factors accounted for 20% of the total 10 flight delay factors. This suggests that

FIGURE 2.78   Step 3 in Section 2.8.

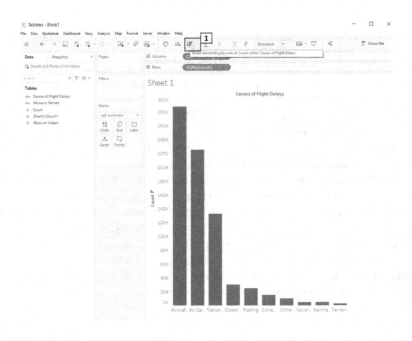

FIGURE 2.79   Step 4 in Section 2.8.

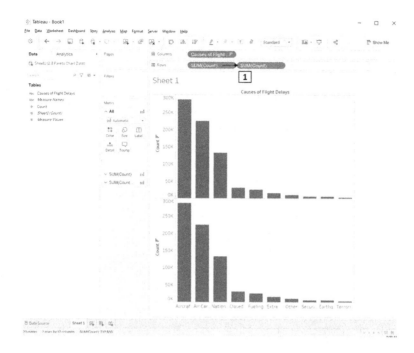

FIGURE 2.80 Step 5 in Section 2.8.

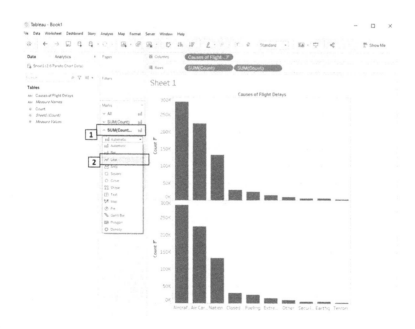

FIGURE 2.81 Step 6 in Section 2.8.

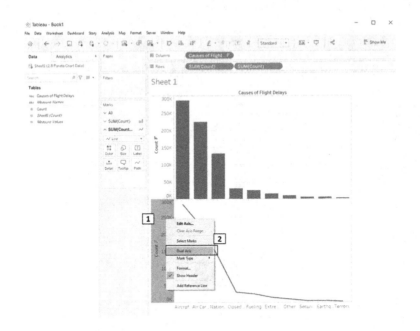

FIGURE 2.82 Step 7 in Section 2.8.

FIGURE 2.83 Step 8 in Section 2.8.

FIGURE 2.84 Step 9 in Section 2.8.

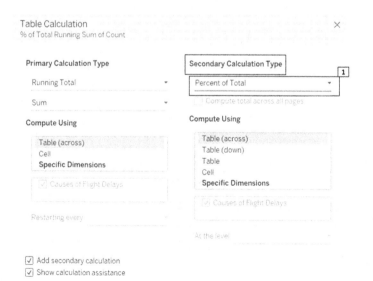

FIGURE 2.85 Step 10 in Section 2.8.

FIGURE 2.86   Step 11 in Section 2.8.

FIGURE 2.87   Step 12 in Section 2.8.

FIGURE 2.88 Step 13 in Section 2.8.

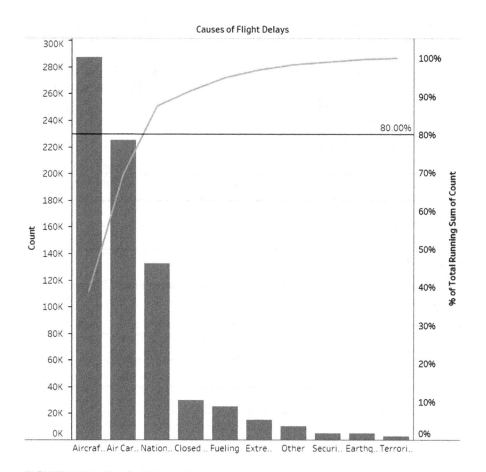

FIGURE 2.89 The final Pareto chart.

improvement effort could be prioritized on air carriers arriving late and air carrier delay issues to have the most significant impact on solving the flight delay issues.

2.9   BUMP CHART

2.9.1   INTRODUCTION OF BUMP CHART

The bump chart is a type of line chart, and it shows the changes in the ranking of multiple items over time. This chart focuses on the relative comparisons among different items. For example, Table 2.18 shows the smartphone quarterly market data between 2018 and 2020.

Each quarter's ranking of shipments could be assigned based on the shipment data, as seen in Table 2.19.

Based on the ranking data, the bump chart could be constructed, as seen in Figure 2.90. The bump chart shows that Samsung was continuously highly ranked (number 1 or 2) over time, indicating that Samsung is a strong leader in the smartphone industry. Apple and Huawei showed some fluctuations in ranking to secure the second or the first place. Huawei's ranking has been increased over the recent three quarters, which could be related to their increased sales in China. Lenovo's ranking has not been changed throughout time. The next section will describe how to use Tableau to construct the bump chart.

2.9.2   TABLEAU EXAMPLE

Table 2.20 shows the millions of passengers carried by airline groups from the year 2011 to 2019. Relative comparisons among airlines would be useful to understand their market share in the world over time. Perform the following steps to construct the bump chart using Tableau.

TABLE 2.18

Smartphone Quarterly Market Data (Global Smartphone Shipments in Millions).

Brands	2018 Q1	2018 Q2	2018 Q3	2018 Q4	2019 Q1	2019 Q2	2019 Q3	2019 Q4	2020 Q1	2020 Q2
Huawei	39.3	54.2	52	59.7	59.1	56.6	66.8	56.2	49	54.8
Samsung	78.2	71.5	72.3	69.8	72	76.3	78.2	70.4	58.6	54.2
Apple	52.2	41.3	46.9	65.9	42	36.5	44.8	72.3	40	37.5
Xiomi	28.1	32	33.3	25.6	27.8	32.3	31.7	32.9	29.7	26.5
Oppo	24.2	29.6	33.9	31.3	25.7	30.6	32.3	31.4	22.3	24.5
Vivo	18.9	26.5	30.5	26.5	23.9	27	31.3	31.5	21.6	22.5
Lenovo	8.6	9	11	10.1	9.5	9.5	10	11.7	5.9	7.5

Adapted from https://report.counterpointresearch.com/posts/report_view/Monitor/2026

TABLE 2.19

Ranking of Smartphone Quarterly Market Data

Brands	2018 Q1	2018 Q2	2018 Q3	2018 Q4	2019 Q1	2019 Q2	2019 Q3	2019 Q4	2020 Q1	2020 Q2
Huawei	3	2	2	3	2	2	2	3	2	1
Samsung	1	1	1	1	1	1	1	2	1	2
Apple	2	3	3	2	3	3	3	1	3	3
Xiomi	4	4	5	6	4	4	5	4	4	4
Oppo	5	5	4	4	5	5	4	6	5	5
Vivo	6	6	6	5	6	6	6	5	6	6
Lenovo	7	7	7	7	7	7	7	7	7	7

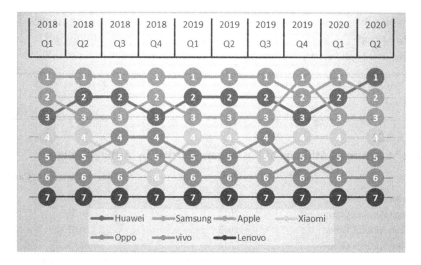

FIGURE 2.90   The bump chart of the smartphone market share.

For Tableau use, the data structure was modified, as seen in Table 2.21. This shows partial data as an example.

Step 1: Open Tableau and click on "Microsoft Excel." Upload the Excel file which contains the data or drag the data file onto the screen to upload it.

Step 2: Once the data file is uploaded, the data is adjusted into columns as shown in Figure 2.91. Then click on "sheet 1" at the bottom.

Step 3: Drag the "Year" measure to the Columns shelf [1] and "Millions of passengers carried" measure to the Rows shelf [2] then drag "Airline" to "Color" in the Marks [3]. Then click "SUM (Millions of passengers

TABLE 2.20
Millions of Passengers Carried by Airline Groups

Airline	2011	2012	2013	2014	2015	2016	2017	2018	2019
American Airlines Group	86.042	86.3	86.823	87.83	146.53	198.7	199.6	203.74	215.18
Delta Air Lines	113.731	117	120.636	129.433	138.842	183.7	186.4	192.46	204
Southwest Airlines	110.587	112	115.323	129.087	144.575	151.8	157.8	163.6	162.68
United Airlines	50.473	92.6	90.161	90.439	95.384	143.2	148.1	158.33	162.44
Ryanair	76.422	79.6	81.395	86.37	101.401	119.8	130.3	139.2	152.4
China Southern Airlines	80.545	86.3	91.504	100.683	109.301	84.9	126.3	139.8	151.63
Lufthansa Group	112	109	110.4	112.5	115.2	117.4	130	142.3	145.2
China Eastern Airlines	73.1	79.6	62.653	66.174	75.139	80.9	110.8	121.1	130
IAG	51.7	54.6	67.2	77.3	94.9	100.7	104.83	112.92	118.3
Air China Group	69.4	72.4	77.7	83	89.8	96.5	101.6	109.7	115

(Adapted from https://en.wikipedia.org/wiki/Largest_airlines_in_the_world)

TABLE 2.21
Data Structure of Millions of Passengers Carried by Airline Groups

Airline	Year	Millions of Passengers Carried
American Airlines Group	2011	86.042
American Airlines Group	2012	86.335
American Airlines Group	2013	86.823
American Airlines Group	2014	87.83

carried)" and select "Quick Table Calculation" – "Rank" [4] as seen in Figure 2.92.

Step 4: Click "SUM (Millions of passengers carried)" and select "Compute Using" – "Airline" as seen in Figure 2.93.

Step 5: Press Ctrl (or Command) and Drag to Drop the "SUM (Millions of passengers carried)" pill in the Rows Shelf to the right. This will duplicate the object with all settings applied (Figure 2.94).

Step 6: To adjust the type and size of the second "SUM (Millions of passengers carried)" chart, change the type of chart as "Circle" [1] and change the size of each circle [2] as desired. Click Label on Marks then check "show mark label" and adjust the alignment [3] as seen in Figure 2.95.

FIGURE 2.91 Step 2 in Section 2.9.

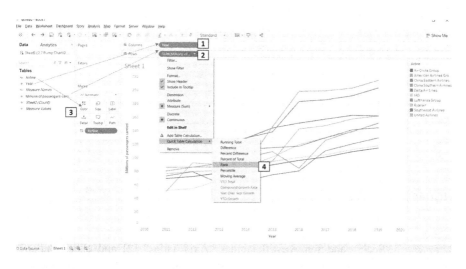

FIGURE 2.92 Step 3 in Section 2.9.

Step 7: Right-click the second pill "SUM(Millions of passengers carried)" in Rows and select Dual Axis (Figure 2.96).

Step 8: To edit the format of the Y-axis for both areas, right-click on the area and select "Edit Axis" then 1) check the "Reversed" box [1] under

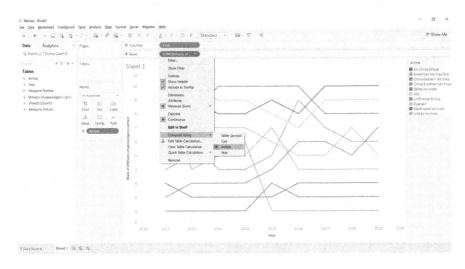

FIGURE 2.93   Step 4 in Section 2.9.

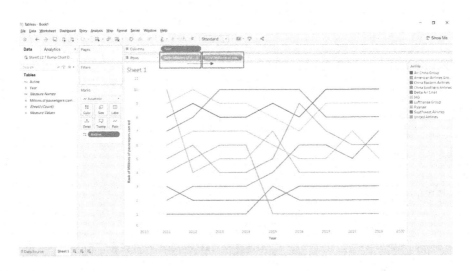

FIGURE 2.94   Step 5 in Section 2.9.

"Scale" and remove title under "Axis Titles" [2] and check "none" under "Major Tick Marks" in the Tick Marks section [3] (Figure 2.97).

Step 9: Final bump chart will be shown (Figure 2.98).

If we look at the bump chart, airlines' ranking in terms of passengers' number has fluctuated between 2011 and 2019. Delta Air Lines has maintained high performance, mainly ranking first and second in the past nine years. Southwest Airlines was also showing stable business results, staying in second and third places for the past nine

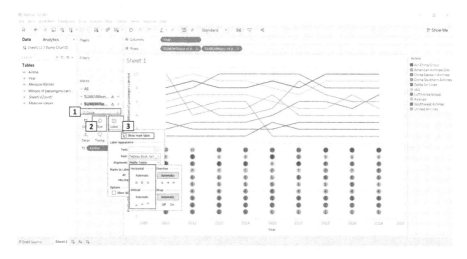

FIGURE 2.95   Step 6 in Section 2.9.

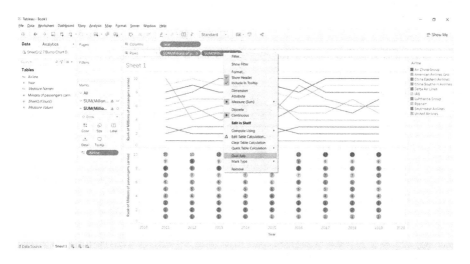

FIGURE 2.96   Step 7 in Section 2.9.

years. From 2011 to 2014, it remained in the 4th to 6th place in the case of American Airlines, then achieved the first place with rapid growth from 2015, keeping the first place so far. China Eastern Airlines, Air China Group, and IAG airlines have been mainly in the lower ranks for nine years.

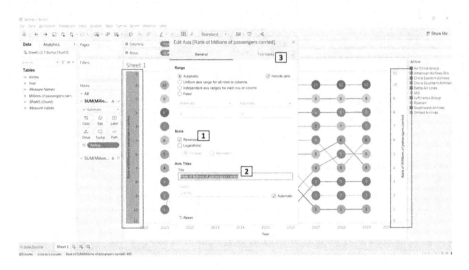

FIGURE 2.97   Step 8 in Section 2.9.

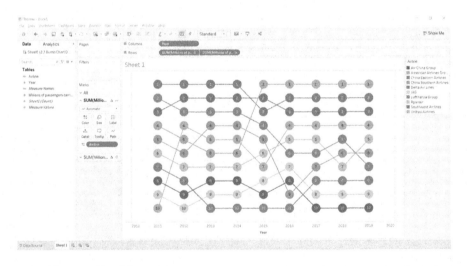

FIGURE 2.98   Final bump chart.

2.10 MAPS

2.10.1 Introduction of Maps

The maps are a useful way to conduct geographic analysis. To visualize the map, the data source needs to have the location (spatial) information (e.g., latitude and longitude coordinates or state names). The map information can be combined with the measures with other types of graphs (e.g., color spectrums, pie charts). The next section will describe how to use Tableau to construct Maps.

2.10.2 Tableau Example

The example is related to the New York city Airbnb data. Table 2.22 shows the 30-sample data, including geographic information (neighborhood, latitude, and longitude), room type, price, and reviews per month. The geographic analysis could be conducted to understand the relative difference in price and reviews among different areas. Perform the following steps to construct the Map using Tableau.

Step 1: Open Tableau and click on "Microsoft Excel." Upload the Excel file which contains the data or drag the data file onto the screen to upload it.

Step 2: Once the data file is uploaded, the data is adjusted into columns then click on "sheet 1" at the bottom.

Step 3: Drag the "Longitude" to the Columns shelf [1] and "Latitude" to the Rows shelf [2]. Then drag "Room Type" to "Color." Drag "Price" measure to "Size" & "Label." Drag "Neighborhood" to "Label" [3]. Since the data is aggregated, click on "analysis" and unselect "aggregate measures" [4] as seen in Figure 2.99.

TABLE 2.22
Sample Data of New York City Airbnb

Neighborhood Group	Neighborhood	Latitude	Longitude	Room Type	Price	Reviews per Month
Brooklyn	Kensington	40.64749	−73.97237	Private room	149	0.21
Manhattan	Midtown	40.75362	−73.98377	Entire home/apt	225	0.38
Manhattan	Harlem	40.80902	−73.9419	Private room	150	
Brooklyn	Clinton Hill	40.68514	−73.95976	Entire home/apt	89	4.64
Manhattan	East Harlem	40.79851	−73.94399	Entire home/apt	80	0.1
Manhattan	Murray Hill	40.74767	−73.975	Entire home/apt	200	0.59
Brooklyn	Bedford–Stuyvesant	40.68688	−73.95596	Private room	60	0.4
Manhattan	Hell's Kitchen	40.76489	−73.98493	Private room	79	3.47
Manhattan	Upper West Side	40.80178	−73.96723	Private room	79	0.99

(Continued)

TABLE 2.22 (Continued)

Neighborhood Group	Neighborhood	Latitude	Longitude	Room Type	Price	Reviews per Month
Manhattan	Chinatown	40.71344	−73.99037	Entire home/apt	150	1.33
Manhattan	Upper West Side	40.80316	−73.96545	Entire home/apt	135	0.43
Manhattan	Hell's Kitchen	40.76076	−73.98867	Private room	85	1.5
Brooklyn	South Slope	40.66829	−73.98779	Private room	89	1.34
Manhattan	Upper West Side	40.79826	−73.96113	Private room	85	0.91
Manhattan	West Village	40.7353	−74.00525	Entire home/apt	120	0.22
Brooklyn	Williamsburg	40.70837	−73.95352	Entire home/apt	140	1.2
Brooklyn	Fort Greene	40.69169	−73.97185	Entire home/apt	215	1.72
Manhattan	Chelsea	40.74192	−73.99501	Private room	140	2.12
Brooklyn	Crown Heights	40.67592	−73.94694	Entire home/apt	99	4.44
Manhattan	East Harlem	40.79685	−73.94872	Entire home/apt	190	
Brooklyn	Williamsburg	40.71842	−73.95718	Entire home/apt	299	0.07
Brooklyn	Park Slope	40.68069	−73.97706	Private room	130	1.09
Brooklyn	Park Slope	40.67989	−73.97798	Private room	80	0.37
Brooklyn	Park Slope	40.68001	−73.97865	Private room	110	0.61
Brooklyn	Bedford–Stuyvesant	40.68371	−73.94028	Entire home/apt	120	0.73
Brooklyn	Windsor Terrace	40.65599	−73.97519	Private room	60	1.37
Manhattan	Inwood	40.86754	−73.92639	Private room	80	
Manhattan	Hell's Kitchen	40.76715	−73.98533	Entire home/apt	150	0.49
Manhattan	Inwood	40.86482	−73.92106	Private room	44	1.11
Manhattan	East Village	40.7292	−73.98542	Entire home/apt	180	0.24

(Adapted from http://insideairbnb.com/)

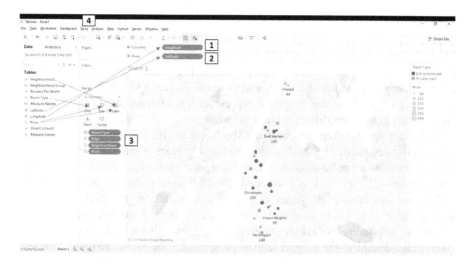

FIGURE 2.99 Step 3 in Section 2.10.

FIGURE 2.100 Step 4 in Section 2.10.

Step 4: To adjust the bubble's size and color opacity, click "Color" [1] and "Size" [2] in the Marks and change them as desired. And the map can be navigated by right-clicking and move after selecting cross-arrow [3] (Figure 2.100).

The map shows that rents for entire houses/apartments tend to be more distributed in southern New York than northern New York. In terms of price, there was no apparent difference between regions. As expected, renting an entire house/apartment forms a higher price point than renting a private room.

2.11 GANTT CHART

2.11.1 INTRODUCTION OF GANTT CHART

Henry Gantt initially developed the Gantt chart in 1910. The objectives of this chart are to effectively plan the course of actions in the project and monitor and control the project's schedule. This graphical representation has been commonly used in project management by different types of businesses.

There are several steps to construct the Gantt chart. A list of tasks needs to be initially designed. For each task, responsible team members are assigned. The order of tasks can be determined, and a separate row is allocated in the chart. The duration of each task is estimated. Possible issues during the project are anticipated and their contingency time can be allocated in the chart. The inter-dependencies of tasks are determined. For instance, task A needs to be complete before the beginning of task B in the project. Once all members agree on the Gantt chart design in the project, actual progress can be monitored and updated on the chart. This chart can also be shared with the stakeholders and other personnel who are interested in the project.

For the visualization, the Gantt chart shows the start and end time of each task. The length of the horizontal bar represents the task duration. The project progress can be assessed by comparing the current time (i.e., vertical line) with the expected end time of a specific task. This helps to judge if current progress is behind, ahead, or on time. The Gantt chart allows seeing when multiple tasks need to be performed at the same time by observing the overlapped parts of horizontal bars. This helps project members to better plan and manage the time and resources in advance. The next section will describe the step-by-step method of constructing the Gantt chart using Tableau.

2.11.2 TABLEAU EXAMPLE

In this example, a project manager manages three team members (John, Paul, and Mike) and planning their schedules across ten tasks. The schedule is regularly updated, and Table 2.23 shows a recent example. The project manager is considering leveraging the data visualization to:

Get a better sense of how this project and members line up.

1. Track progress to completion for each task.
2. Share an intuitive schedule update with three team members.

Perform the following steps to construct the Gantt chart using Tableau.

Step 1: Open Tableau and click on "Microsoft Excel." Upload the Excel file which contains the data or drag the data file onto the screen to upload it.
Step 2: Once the data file is uploaded, the data is adjusted into columns. Then click on "sheet 1" at the bottom (Figure 2.101).
Step 3: Place the cursor on the blank space below the "measure values" on the

TABLE 2.23

Example of the Project Schedule

Project	Start Date	End Date	In-Charge	Percentage Complete
Task 1	6/12/20	8/1/20	John	100
Task 2	7/5/20	8/14/20	Paul	100
Task 3	8/8/20	9/27/20	Paul	90
Task 4	9/19/20	11/18/20	John	50
Task 5	9/21/20	12/10/20	Mike	20
Task 6	10/5/20	11/14/20	Mike	15
Task 7	10/7/20	10/24/20	John	5
Task 8	11/6/20	11/26/20	John	0
Task 9	12/12/20	1/1/21	Paul	0
Task 10	1/12/21	3/13/21	Mike	0

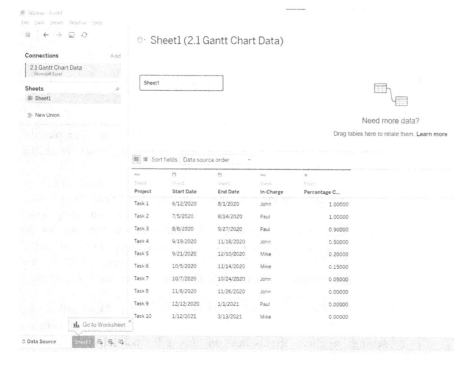

FIGURE 2.101 Step 2 in Section 2.11.

screen's left side and right-click of "Create Calculated Field" (Figure 2.102).

Step 4: Enter the title as "Duration." Enter the calculations "DATEDIFF ("day", [Start Date], [End Date])" as shown in Figure 2.103. Apply it and click OK.

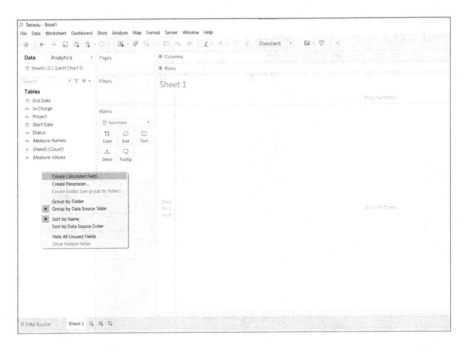

FIGURE 2.102   Step 3 in Section 2.11.

Step 4: Select "Create Calculated Field" and enter the title as "Completed."
Enter the calculations "[Duration]*[Percentage Complete]" as shown
in Figure 2.104. Apply it and click OK.

Step 5: First, drag the "Start Date" dimension to the Columns shelf [1] as seen
in Figure 2.105. On the Columns shelf, click the "Year (Start Date)"
drop-down arrow, and then select "Day." In the same drop-down
arrow, also select "Continuous." Second, drag the "project" to the
rows shelf [2] as shown in Figure 2.105. Lastly, drag "duration" to the
"size" [3]. To get the Gantt Chart's entire view, click on the
"Standard" drop-down arrow, located on the top toolbar, and then
select "Entire View."

Step 6: Press Ctrl (or Command) and Drag to Drop the "Day" pill in the
Columns Shelf to the right. This will duplicate the object with all
settings applied. Right-click on this pill and select Dual Axis
(Figure 2.106).

Step 7: Right-click on the Axis Header and select "Synchronize Axis"
(Figure 2.107).

Step 8: In the second "DAY" Marks Panel, drag "Completed" onto the "Size"
Mark. Click on the "Color" Mark and set different colors (e.g., Orange or
green) (Figure 2.108).

Step 9: In the first "DAY" Marks Panel, drag "Percentage Complete" onto the

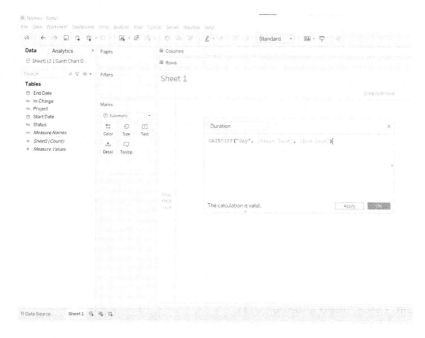

FIGURE 2.103   Step 4 in Section 2.11.

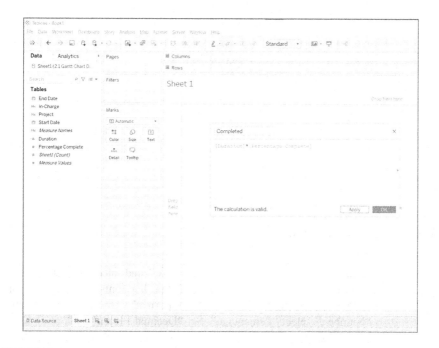

FIGURE 2.104   Step 4 in Section 2.11.

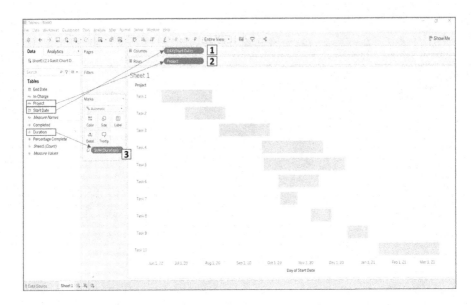

FIGURE 2.105   Step 5 in Section 2.11.

FIGURE 2.106   Step 6 in Section 2.11.

"Label" Mark (Figure 2.109). Click "Label" and select the "Alignment" drop-down menu. Set "center" in the horizontal. Right-click on "Percentage Complete" and select "Format". Under "Default" and "Number," select "Percentage". Set "Decimal Places" as 0.

Step 10: Add a filter to the "In-charge" of tasks. Drag "In-charge" to the filters

FIGURE 2.107 Step 7 in Section 2.11.

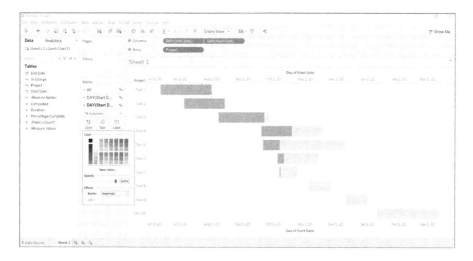

FIGURE 2.108 Step 8 in Section 2.11.

shelf and check all the boxes in the pop-up window. Apply and click OK (Figure 2.110).

Step 11: On the filter shelf, click drop-down arrow and select "Show Filter". The filter will be shown on the right side of the screen. By checking/unchecking the boxes, we can filter the in-charge persons as shown in Figure 2.111.

Step 12: Create a calculated field that returns today's date to use as a reference line (Figure 2.112). The calculated field is named "Today's Date" and enter [Today ()]. Drag "Today's Date" to "Detail" on the first Marks. Right-click "Today's Date" on the Marks and select "Exact Date".

FIGURE 2.109   Step 9 in Section 2.11.

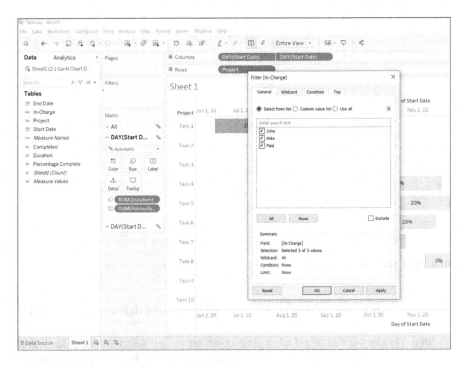

FIGURE 2.110   Step 10 in Section 2.11.

FIGURE 2.111   Step 11 in Section 2.11.

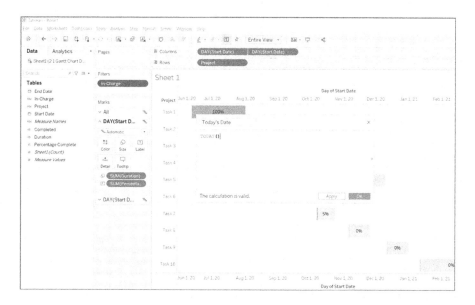

FIGURE 2.112   Step 12 in Section 2.11.

Step 13: Right-click the date axis and select "Add Reference Line" (Figure 2.113).

Step 14: In the "Add Reference Line, Band, or Box dialog", for "Value", select "Today's Date" from the drop-down menu. Format the reference line as desired (Figure 2.114).

Step 15: Final Gantt chart is shown (Figure 2.115).

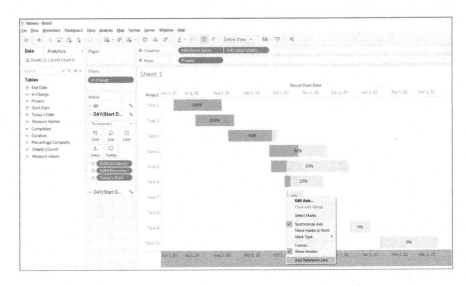

FIGURE 2.113   Step 13 in Section 2.11.

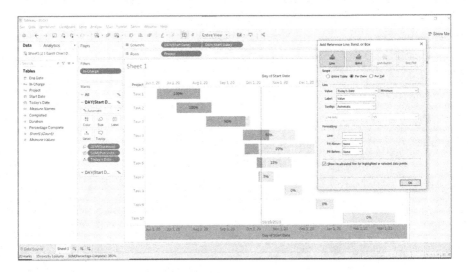

FIGURE 2.114   Step 14 in Section 2.11.

Based on the Gantt chart, we can see that as of October 10, 2020, Tasks 1 and 2 were completed as planned, and only 90% of Task 3 was completed. In other words, 10% of Task 3 was behind schedule. For Task 4, the work's progress is ahead of the expected schedule, and for Task 5, it is slightly behind the expected schedule.

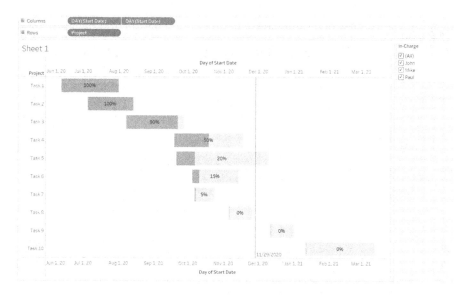

FIGURE 2.115 Final Gantt chart.

2.12 CONTROL CHART FOR VARIABLES

2.12.1 INTRODUCTION OF CONTROL CHART FOR VARIABLES

The control chart is a type of line chart over the process flow (e.g., time). On top of that, the average horizontal line is displayed to understand the overall mean of the process's quality characteristics. Based on this centreline (i.e., average line), we can identify how individual data deviates from the centreline, which indicates the variation of the process. To identify any unusual behavior of the process, upper and lower control limits are displayed on the chart. These control limits are typically set as ± 3 × standard deviations. If any data point is outside the control limits, we consider this data is out-of-control. In this case, the investigation (root cause analysis) is needed to identify the issue's potential causes.

Table 2.24 shows the sample data of the thickness (mm) of the manufacturing plant's part. Quality engineers wanted to evaluate whether the process is stable or not. Three parts were randomly collected, and their thickness was measured over ten days.

In this case, we could apply X-bar and R charts, which is one type of control charts for variables. The "X-bar" is the average of values per sample. For each sample, there were three measurements. The average of these measurements is summarized in Table 2.25. The "R" is the range of values per sample. In other words, the difference between the maximum and minimum values per sample. The R values are summarized in Table 2.25. For the next step, the total average of each "X-bar" and "R" could be computed, respectively, as seen in Table 2.25.

The next step is to determine the control limits of the process. For the X-bar chart, the control limits can be calculated using Equations 2.4 and 2.5. It determines

TABLE 2.24

Thickness (mm) of the Part Produced in the Manufacturing Plant

	Thickness (mm)		
Sample	1	2	3
1	30	44	19
2	28	26	21
3	60	70	85
4	22	34	28
5	49	50	8
6	52	48	11
7	90	51	6
8	51	43	12
9	17	32	24
10	11	28	18

TABLE 2.25

Thickness (mm) of the Part Produced in the Manufacturing Plant

	Thickness (mm)				
Sample	1	2	3	X-bar	R
1	30	44	19	31	25
2	28	26	21	25	7
3	60	70	85	71.7	25
4	22	34	28	28	12
5	49	50	8	35.7	42
6	52	48	11	37	41
7	90	51	6	49	84
8	51	43	12	35.3	39
9	17	32	24	24.3	15
10	11	28	18	19	17
			Total Average	35.6	30.7

the control limits as 3 × standard deviations from the centreline. To increase the efficiency of the computation, constants (e.g., A_2) are provided.

$$UCL_{\bar{x}} = \bar{\bar{x}} + 3\frac{\hat{\sigma}}{\sqrt{n}} = \bar{\bar{x}} + A_2\bar{R} \tag{2.4}$$

TABLE 2.26
Constants Used for the X-bar and R Charts

Subgroup	X-bar Chart	R Chart	
	A_2	D_3	D_4
2	1.880	0	3.267
3	1.023	0	2.574
4	0.729	0	2.282
5	0.577	0	2.114
6	0.483	0	2.004

$$LCL_{\bar{x}} = \bar{\bar{x}} - 3\frac{\hat{\sigma}}{\sqrt{n}} = \bar{\bar{x}} - A_2\bar{R} \qquad (2.5)$$

Table 2.26 shows an example of the constants table. Depending on the sample size (subgroup size), an appropriate constant can be selected. In our example, the subgroup size is 3, so A2 = 1.023.

By applying the Equations 2.6 and 2.7 and A_2, the upper control limit (UCL) is 67.0 and the lower control limit (LCL) is 4.19.

$$UCL_{\bar{x}} = 35.6 + 1.023 \times 30.7 = 67.0 \qquad (2.6)$$

$$UCL_{\bar{x}} = 35.6 - 1.023 \times 30.7 = 4.19 \qquad (2.7)$$

If we plot the results, the X-bar chart could be displayed as seen in Figure 2.116. The centerline indicates the total average of the X-bar values. Each data point represents the X-bar value per sample. We could detect that the sample 3 data point is

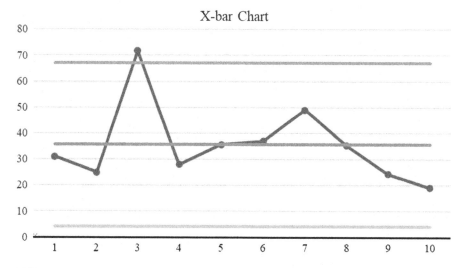

FIGURE 2.116 The X-bar chart of the thickness (mm) of the parts.

above the upper control limit. The thickness measured on day 3 highly deviates from the centerline. This unusual data implies that some errors of the process could occur on day 3. The investigation would be necessary to identify the issue and improve the process.

Like the X-bar chart approach, we could also construct the R chart. Equations 2.8 and 2.9 shows how to compute the control limits of the R chart. For computational efficiency, constant values are provided as seen in above Table 2.26. In this case, separate constant values (D4 and D3) are applied to upper and lower control limits.

$$UCL_{\bar{R}} = D_4 \bar{R} \tag{2.8}$$

$$LCL_{\bar{R}} = D_3 \bar{R} \tag{2.9}$$

In our example with the subgroup size 3, the Equations 2.10 and 2.11 could be applied to compute the control limits.

$$UCL_{\bar{R}} = 2.574 \times 30.7 = 79.0 \tag{2.10}$$

$$LCL_{\bar{R}} = 0 \tag{2.11}$$

If we plot the results, the R chart could be shown in Figure 2.117. The centerline indicates the total average of range (R) values. Each data point represents the R values per sample. We could detect that the sample 7 value is above the upper control limit. In other words, there was an excessive difference between the three values measured on day 7. This inconsistency could be related to some errors of the parts, measurement systems, or workers. An immediate investigation would be needed to solve the issue. The next section will describe how to use Tableau to construct the X-bar and R control charts.

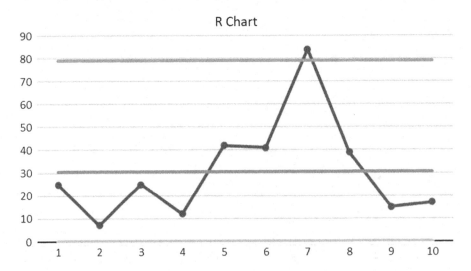

FIGURE 2.117 The R chart of the thickness (mm) of the parts.

TABLE 2.27
Length (cm) of the Part Produced in the Assembly Line

Sample	Subgroup					
	1	2	3	4	5	6
1	9.14	9.11	10.16	9.69	10.03	10.34
2	10.44	10.45	10.76	10.78	9.97	10.86
3	9.70	9.57	9.91	9.95	9.12	9.05
4	9.37	10.50	9.76	10.71	9.48	9.87
5	9.92	9.31	10.56	10.68	9.46	9.58
6	9.01	10.14	9.87	9.12	10.69	10.40
7	9.01	10.87	9.05	9.91	9.88	10.17
8	9.49	10.92	9.59	9.46	10.45	9.03
9	10.19	9.64	9.76	9.39	10.08	10.05
10	10.32	9.37	9.51	10.16	10.07	9.30
11	9.63	9.50	10.56	9.17	9.15	9.46
12	10.55	9.34	10.73	9.39	9.32	10.43
13	9.06	9.36	9.43	9.93	10.89	9.13
14	10.81	9.37	9.30	10.93	9.52	9.50
15	10.19	10.19	10.66	9.99	9.53	10.50
16	9.38	10.26	10.43	9.71	9.20	10.06
17	10.04	9.22	9.22	9.67	9.66	9.06
18	9.41	9.97	10.03	10.58	9.96	10.09
19	9.29	9.21	10.23	9.13	9.23	10.10
20	10.17	10.51	9.82	9.88	10.50	9.86

2.12.2 TABLEAU EXAMPLE

Table 2.27 shows the length (cm) of the part produced in the assembly line. For each day, six parts were randomly selected, and the operator measured their length. This data collection was continuously performed over 20 days. The quality engineer wants to determine whether the process is in control. Perform the following steps to construct the X-bar and R charts using Tableau.

For the convenient use of Tableau, the data structure was modified as seen in Table 2.28. The R chart will be constructed first, and then the X-bar chart will be developed subsequently.

2.12.3 R CHART

Step 1: Open Tableau and click on "Microsoft Excel." Upload the Excel file which contains the data or drag the data file onto the screen to upload it.
Step 2: Once the data file is uploaded, the data is adjusted into columns. Then click on "sheet 1" at the bottom.

TABLE 2.28

Data Structure of the Length (cm) of the Part Produced in the Assembly Line

Sample	Subgroup	Length
1	1	9.14
1	2	9.11
1	3	10.16
1	4	9.69
1	5	10.03

Step 3: Place the cursor on the blank space below the "measure values" on the screen's left side and right-click and select "Create Calculated Field." Then create three measures including LCL_R, UCL_R, and Range as shown in Figure 2.118. The 0 indicates D3 and 2.004 indicates D4 constants as shown in previous Table 2.26.

1. **Range**
   MAX([Length]) – MIN([Length])
2. **LCL_R**
   0*WINDOW_AVG([Range])
3. **UCL_R**
   2.004*WINDOW_AVG([Range])

FIGURE 2.118   Step 3 in Section 2.12.

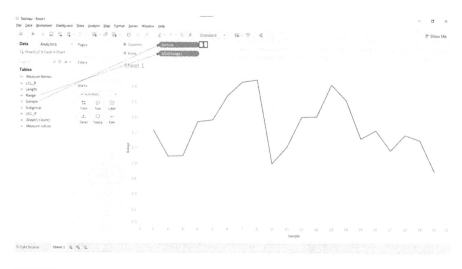

FIGURE 2.119   Step 4 in Section 2.12.

Step 4: Drag the "Sample" measure to the Columns shelf and change it from "measure" to "dimension" [1]. Drag "Range" measure to the Rows shelf as seen in Figure 2.119.

Step 5: Right-click on the right side y-axis and select "Add reference line". Select AGG(Range) in the dropdown menu under "Line" and "Value" (Figure 2.120).

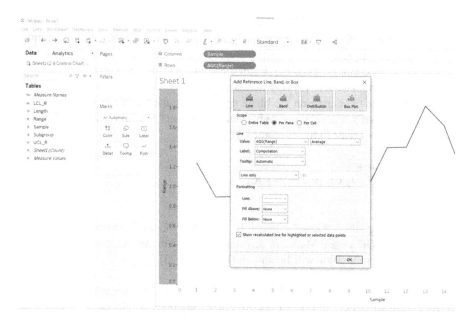

FIGURE 2.120   Step 5 in Section 2.12.

FIGURE 2.121   Step 6 in Section 2.12.

Step 6: Drag the "LCL_R" and "UCL_R" measures to the Marks. Right-click on the right side y-axis and select "Add reference line." Select "UCL_R" in the dropdown menu under "Line" and "Value". Apply the same procedure for "LCL_R" (Figure 2.121).

Step 7: Press Ctrl (or Command) and Drag to Drop the "AGG(Range)" pill in the Rows Shelf to the right [1]. This will duplicate the object with all settings applied. Change the type of chart as "Line" for the first "AGG(Range)" and as "Circle" for the second one in the Marks [2]. Right-click on this pill and select Dual Axis [3]. Right-click on the left side y-axis and select "Synchronize Axis" [4]. Right-click on the right side y-axis and uncheck "Show Header" [5] (Figure 2.122).

Step 8: Place the cursor on the blank space below the "measure values" on the screen's left side and right-click and select "Create Calculated Field". Then create "Out-of-control_R" measure.

Out-of-control_R
[Range] < [LCL_R] OR [Range] > [UCL_R]

Step 9: Drag the "Out-of-control_R" to the "Color" under the second AGG(Range) Mark. If any data point outside the control limits, a different color will be shown (Figure 2.123).

Based on the R chart, there were no out-of-control points. In other words, there was no excessive variability of the part length among six parts within each sample. For the range of the length of the part, this process is in statistical control.

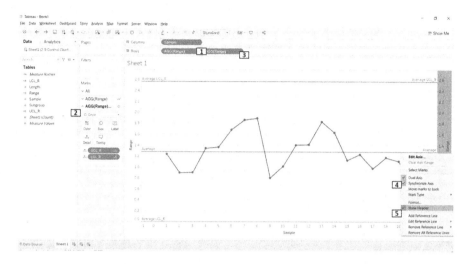

FIGURE 2.122 Step 7 in Section 2.12.

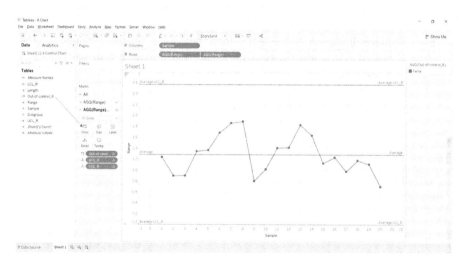

FIGURE 2.123 Step 9 in Section 2.12.

2.12.4 X-BAR CHART

Step 1: Create "Sheet 2" at the bottom panel.

Step 2: Drag the "Sample" measure to the Columns shelf and change it from "measure" to "dimension" [1]. Drag "Length" measure to the Rows shelf and change it as AVG(Length) [2]. Then right-click in the left Y-

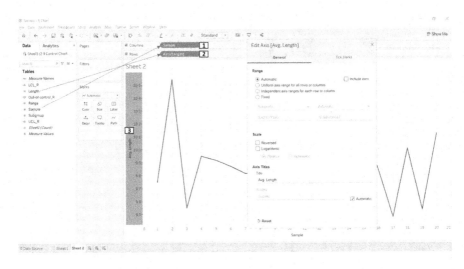

FIGURE 2.124   X-bar chart Step 2 in Section 2.12.

axis to uncheck "include zero" in the "Edit Axis[Avg.Length]" [3] as seen in Figure 2.124.

Step 3: Place the cursor on the blank space below the "measure values" on the screen's left side and right-click and select "Create Calculated Field." Then create two measures including LCL_X-bar [1] and UCL_X-bar [2] as shown in Figure 2.125. The 0.483 indicates A2 constant, as shown in the previous Table 2.26.

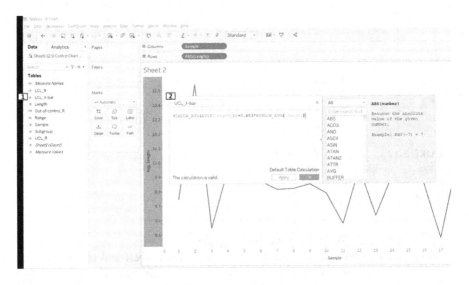

FIGURE 2.125   X-bar chart Step 3 in Section 2.12.

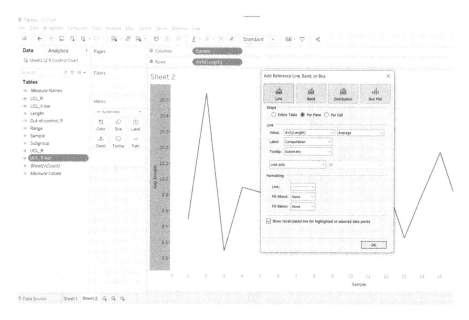

FIGURE 2.126 X-bar chart Step 4 in Section 2.12.

1. LCL_X-bar
   WINDOW_AVG(AVG([Length])) − 0.483*WINDOW_AVG([Range])
2. UCL_X-bar
   WINDOW_AVG(AVG([Length])) + 0.483*WINDOW_AVG([Range])

Step 4: Right-click on the y-axis and select "Add reference line". Select AVG(Length) in the dropdown menu under "Line" and "Value" (Figure 2.126).

Step 5: Drag the "LCL_X-bar" and "UCL_X-bar" measures to the Marks. Right-click on the right side y-axis and select "Add reference line". Select "UCL_X-bar" in the dropdown menu under "Line" and "Value". Apply the same procedure for "LCL_X-bar"(Figure 2.127).

Step 6: Press Ctrl (or Command) and Drag to Drop the "AVG(Length)" pill in the Rows Shelf to the right [1]. This will duplicate the object with all settings applied. Change the type of chart as "Line" for the first "AVG(Length)" and as "Circle" for the second one in the Marks [2]. Right-click on this pill and select Dual Axis [3]. Right-click on the left side y-axis and select "Synchronize Axis" [4]. Right-click on the right side y-axis and uncheck "Show Header" [5] (Figure 2.128).

Step 7: Place the cursor on the blank space below the "measure values" on the screen's left side and right-click and select "Create Calculated

FIGURE 2.127   X-bar chart Step 5 in Section 2.12.

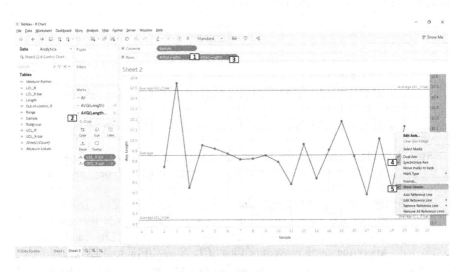

FIGURE 2.128   X-bar chart Step 6 in Section 2.12.

Field". Then create "Out-of-control_X-bar" measure as shown in Figure 2.129.

Out-of-control_X-bar
AVG([Length]) < [LCL_X-bar] OR AVG([Length]) > [UCL_X-bar]

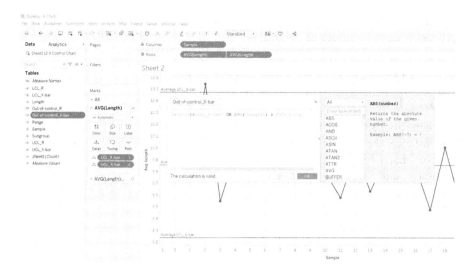

FIGURE 2.129 X-bar chart Step 7 in Section 2.12.

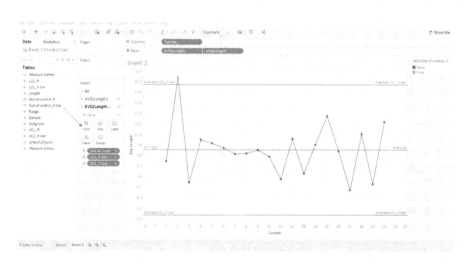

FIGURE 2.130 X-bar chart Step 8 in Section 2.12.

Step 8: Drag the "Out-of-control_X-bar" to the "Color" under the second AVG(Length) Mark. If any data point outside the control limits, the different colors will be shown (Figure 2.130).

Based on the X-bar chart, sample 2 was out-of-control. Sample 2's part length was higher than the upper control limit. This indicates that sample 2 showed an unusually long length compared to the part length from the normal process. The investigation would be necessary to find assignable causes of the issues. The process is considered out of control.

2.13   CONTROL CHART FOR ATTRIBUTES

2.13.1   INTRODUCTION OF CONTROL CHART FOR ATTRIBUTES

The control chart for attributes is to monitor categorical or qualitative variables. For instance, the number of defective items could be considered as an attribute. Control charts for attributes include p chart, np chart, c chart, and u chart. This section could focus on the p chart, which monitors the proportion of non-conforming or defective items. The centreline of the p chart is p-bar, which is computed using Equation 2.12.

$$\bar{p} = \frac{total \ number \ of \ defective}{total \ number \ of \ samples} \tag{2.12}$$

Like the x-bar and R charts, upper and lower control limits of the p chart can be established using Equations 2.13 and 2.14.

$$UCL = \bar{p} + 3\sqrt{\frac{\bar{p}(1 - \bar{p})}{n}} \tag{2.13}$$

$$LCL = \bar{p} - 3\sqrt{\frac{\bar{p}(1 - \bar{p})}{n}} \tag{2.14}$$

Table 2.29 shows the example of the number of defective items over ten days. For each day, 100 samples were randomly collected, and the defective items

TABLE 2.29
Number of Defective Items Counted per Day

Day	Number of Defective	Sample Size
1	7	100
2	8	100
3	15	100
4	12	100
5	10	100
6	52	100
7	9	100
8	11	100
9	16	100
10	13	100

were counted. The p chart could be used to determine whether the process is in control.

First, the p-bar or centreline could be computed using Equation 2.15.

$$\bar{p} = \frac{total \ \ number \ \ of \ \ defective}{total \ \ number \ \ of \ \ samples} = \frac{153}{1000} = 0.153 \qquad (2.15)$$

Based on the p-bar value, the upper and lower control limits can be computed using Equations 2.16 and 2.17. The LCL was initially computed as −0.189. Since negative values of defectives are not realistic, the LCL value could be bounded as 0.

$$UCL = 0.153 + 3\sqrt{\frac{0.153(1 - 0.153)}{100}} = 0.495 \qquad (2.16)$$

$$LCL = 0.153 - 3\sqrt{\frac{0.153(1 - 0.153)}{100}} = -0.189 => 0 \qquad (2.17)$$

For the last step, we could calculate the p value (proportion) for each day as seen in Table 2.30. For example, day 1's p value is calculated using Equation 2.18.

$$p_1 = \frac{7}{100} = 0.07 \qquad (2.18)$$

Figure 2.131 shows the p chart from the example. Each data point represents the p value of each day. It shows that day 6 has an out-of-control point. There was an unusual proportion of defective (52%). This could be investigated to find the

TABLE 2.30
The Number of Defective Items Counted Per Day

Day	Number of Defective	Sample Size	p (proportion)
1	7	100	0.07
2	8	100	0.08
3	15	100	0.15
4	12	100	0.12
5	10	100	0.1
6	52	100	0.52
7	9	100	0.09
8	11	100	0.11
9	16	100	0.16
10	13	100	0.13

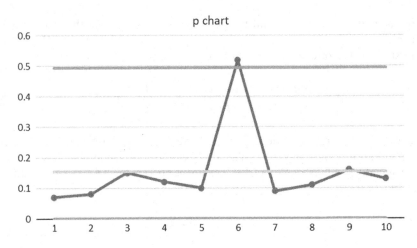

FIGURE 2.131 The p chart of the example.

assignable cause of the issue. The next section will describe how to use Tableau to construct the p chart.

2.13.2 TABLEAU EXAMPLE

Table 2.31 shows the number of defective invoices in the accounting group. This data was collected over 20 days. For each day, 100 invoices were randomly chosen, and the number of defectives was counted. If the invoice has any incorrect information, the invoice was categorized as defective. The quality analyst wants to determine whether the processing of invoices is in control. Perform the following steps to construct the p chart using Tableau.

Step 1: Open Tableau and click on "Microsoft Excel". Upload the Excel file which contains the data or drag the data file onto the screen to upload it.

Step 2: Once the data file is uploaded, the data is adjusted into columns. Then click on "sheet 1" at the bottom.

Step 3: Place the cursor on the blank space below the "measure values" on the screen's left side and right-click and select "Create Calculated Field." Then create p as shown in Figure 2.132.

P

[Number of defective]/[Number of Invoices Inspected]

TABLE 2.31

Number of Defective Invoices in the Accounting Group

Day	Number of Defective	Number of Invoices Inspected
1	21	100
2	25	100
3	17	100
4	32	100
5	24	100
6	26	100
7	21	100
8	60	100
9	29	100
10	22	100
11	24	100
12	31	100
13	26	100
14	31	100
15	27	100
16	18	100
17	29	100
18	24	100
19	24	100
20	20	100

FIGURE 2.132 Step 3 in Section 2.13.

Step 4: Drag the "Day" measure to the Columns shelf [1]. Drag "P" measure to the Rows shelf [2] then change both from "measure" to "dimension" as seen in Figure 2.133.

Step 5: Right-click on the left side y-axis [1] and select "Add reference line." Select P in the dropdown menu under "Line" and "Value". The average of P (P-bar) is shown as 0.2655 (Figure 2.134).

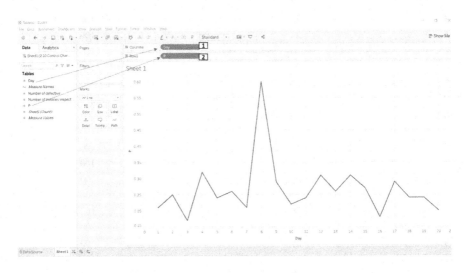

FIGURE 2.133 Step 4 in Section 2.13.

FIGURE 2.134 Step 5 in Section 2.13.

FIGURE 2.135 Step 6 in Section 2.13.

Step 6: Place the cursor on the blank space below the "measure values" on the screen's left side and right-click and select "Create Calculated Field." Then create 2 measures including LCL [1] and UCL [2] as shown in Figure 2.135. The p-bar value (0.2655) found from the previous step was used as a constant. A sample size 100 was used.

1. **LCL**
   0.2655 − 3*SQRT(0.2655*(1 − 0.2655)/100)
2. **UCL**
   0.2655 + 3*SQRT(0.2655*(1 − 0.2655)/100)

Step 7: Drag the "LCL" and "UCL" measures to the Marks. Right-click on the right side y-axis and select "Add reference line" [1]. Select "UCL" in the dropdown menu under "Line" and "Value". Apply the same procedure for "LCL" [2] (Figure 2.136).

Step 8: Press Ctrl (or Command) and Drag to Drop the "P" pill in the Rows Shelf to the right [1]. This will duplicate the object with all settings applied. Change the type of chart as "Line" for the second "P" and as "Circle" for the second one in the Marks [2]. Right-click on this pill and select Dual Axis [3]. Right-click on the left side y-axis and select "Synchronize Axis" [4]. Right-click on the right side y-axis and uncheck "Show Header" [5] (Figure 2.137).

Step 9: Place the cursor on the blank space below the "measure values" on the screen's left side and right-click and select "Create Calculated Field." Then create an "Out-of-control" measure as shown in Figure 2.138.

FIGURE 2.136 Step 7 in Section 2.13.

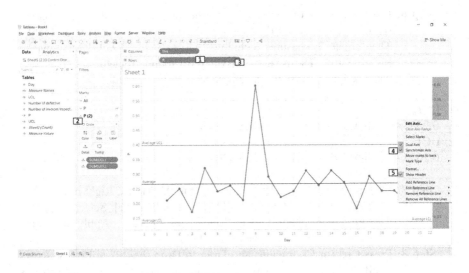

FIGURE 2.137 Step 8 in Section 2.13.

Out-of-control
AVG([P]) < [LCL] OR AVG([P]) > [UCL]

Step 10: Drag the "Out-of-control" to the "Color" under second p Mark. If any data point outside the control limits, different color will be shown (Figure 2.139).

FIGURE 2.138 Step 9 in Section 2.13.

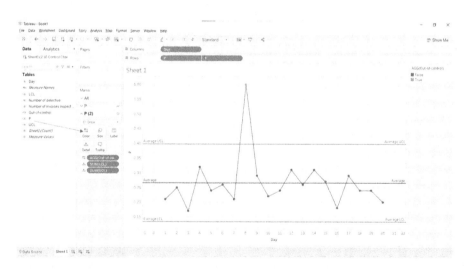

FIGURE 2.139 Step 10 in Section 2.13.

Based on the p chart, there was an out-of-control point. Sample 8's number of defective invoices was higher than the upper control limit. This indicates that day 8's number of defective invoices was unusually high compared to other days. The investigation could be needed to identify the possible causes of this issue, which would be critical to improving the process.

NOTE

1 https://help.tableau.com/current/pro/desktop/en-us/data_structure_for_analysis.htm

REFERENCE

Acharya, M. S., Armaan, A., & Antony, A. S. (2019). A comparison of regression models for prediction of graduate admissions. *2019 International Conference on Computational Intelligence in Data Science (ICCIDS)* (pp. 1–5). IEEE.

3 Quality Dashboard

CHAPTER OVERVIEW AND EXPECTED LEARNING OUTCOMES

In this chapter, we will introduce the basic concepts and potential benefits of using the dashboard in Tableau. Especially, we will discuss different types of the dashboard and suggested design approach to build a dashboard that conveys good data storytelling effectively. We will describe several quality dashboard examples in various industry and step-by-step instructions for using Tableau will be provided. Interpretation of individual plots and dashboards will also be provided to promote critical thinking.

After studying this chapter, expected learning outcomes are:

1. Explain the basic concepts and strengths of using the dashboard.
2. Understand different types of dashboards and design approaches.
3. Know how to use Tableau to construct a quality dashboard of different industries.
4. Interpret charts and dashboards to gain great insights from the data.

3.1 WHAT IS A DASHBOARD?

The coronavirus pandemic caused much suffering, but paradoxically, it was an opportunity to awaken the importance of the dashboard. If we search "COVID" in Google, the line chart and map chart appear at the top of the website. In addition to a line chart showing the number of confirmed patients changing every day, the number of COVID-19 cases by region could be intuitively grasped through a map chart. It suggests that the dashboard has been a very effective tool for comprehensively understanding the state of infectious diseases and COVID-19 vaccine that change every day. Even ordinary people who do not know the exact meaning of the dashboard were able to track the status of the COVID-19 outbreak by checking the dashboard daily with their computer or smartphone.

Tableau's dashboard is a great visualization tool that brings together several charts to make it easier to understand data analysis results. In addition, various charts can be interactively changed according to the purpose by utilizing various functions such as a filtering check box and a slide bar. Through the dashboard, the comprehensive analysis of the data can be performed flexibly, which can improve the understanding and communication of the data with the audience and provide an excellent opportunity for in-depth analysis and discussion.

In many cases, users will need to visualize multiple data on one screen to communicate using data. In this case, Tableau allows users to communicate by expressing multiple data visualizations on one dashboard easily. Dashboards in Tableau are collections of views, filters, parameters, images, and various objects. In order to tell a story using data, there are cases where it is necessary to use e-view, filter, parameter, and image at the same time, and a dashboard is suitable for this. Dashboards allow end-users to explore data interactively and from multiple perspectives.

The dashboard serves a wide variety of purposes and can be tailored according to the circumstance, purpose, and taste of individual users. Dashboards are widely used in industrial sites, and representative examples are as follows:

1. The number of customer calls handled by each employee in the call center, complaints received, and the progress of resolution are monitored by each call center or head office using a dashboard.
2. Global manufacturers manage the operation status of their production operations all over the world through a dashboard. They develop a dashboard to monitor key indicators such as the utilization rate, defect rate, and material supply status and improve efficiency.
3. Utility companies such as electricity and water use a system that enables an immediate response in case of emergency by developing key indicators such as the utilization rate and defect rate of the infrastructure they have and operating as dashboards and monitoring them 24 hours a day.

In the past, before data visualization tools such as Tableau were distributed, a large-scale capital was invested in developing a monitoring system including dashboards. Still, now anyone can create and utilize dashboards intuitively and easily using Tableau.

3.2   DASHBOARD TYPE

There are three common types of dashboards – Operational dashboards, Analytical dashboards, and Strategic dashboards. In order to select a dashboard that suits your purpose, let us look at what types of dashboards are there and select the appropriate type of dashboard.

- **Operational dashboards**
  The operational dashboard is the most common dashboard type. This dashboard type is popular in call center, manufacturing facilities, or project management, and global operations. An operational dashboard is designed to show a comprehensive snapshot of the performance for users. Since the user is not allowed to manipulate data, the user's main purpose is to view the data in a dashboard to understand the overall status and take appropriate actions.

- **Analytical dashboards**
  Analytical dashboards are used when users want to identify trends based on past data and when users want to make decisions based on the analysis results. Contrasting and comparing data across multiple variables are important in analyzing data. Through comparative analysis between data, users could identify correlations, differences, and trends between data, and gain insights in identifying and solving problems. The analytical dashboard can show the data analysis

results on a single screen. Through this, users can suggest the direction for the entire organization to develop.

- **Strategic dashboards**
  Strategic dashboards provide information to measure and track a team or organization's performance based on defined key performance indicators. The strategic dashboard can be used to achieve goals by using the historical performance data as benchmark performance data and comparing data collected from various sources. From the standpoint of managers or executives, it is actively utilized because it can promote continuous development by evaluating the organization's performance and sharing it with the entire organization.

3.3   DASHBOARD DESIGN APPROACH

There are several approaches and principles to building a dashboard, depending on the purpose. The most important step in designing a dashboard is identifying the people who will be shared by the dashboard and knowing what value to deliver to them. If we understand the background and level of understanding of the target audience, we can create a worthwhile design. In order to effectively present and communicate information through the dashboard, the following points could be considered. If so, the dashboard can clearly show the necessary information and the audience understands its intention within a few seconds of seeing it.

- **Priority**
  A common mistake when designing a dashboard is to show that all information is of equal importance. If you want to show the priority of the importance of the data, the widget size and position of the content should be used carefully. Find out the importance of each piece of information and understand which information is most important. It is a good idea to place the most important information in the upper left corner and less and less important information in the lower right corner.

- **Simplicity**
  The real purpose of a dashboard is to present complex information in an easy understanding. Do not show too much information to users. You should also write down the number of lines showing information. If there is any overlapping content, please organize it to not to look cluttered and display the data neatly.

- **Consistency**
  Dashboards look better when you use a consistent layout. Use visually similar elements and layouts to make the dashboard easier to identify. It is good to keep relevant information close to each other and group similar content into visual groups.

- **Proximity**

  Displaying relevant information together on a dashboard makes it easier for users to understand. Do not scatter related information all over the dashboard, and visually group information within the dashboard for easy viewing.

- **Alignment**

  An unaligned look does not make a good impression on users because it feels like the design is less. The elements on the dashboard need to be visually aligned to make the overall look balanced. Align the elements of your dashboard well with each other to make them more organized. It is okay to arrange the widgets on the dashboard in a grid.

- **The beauty of white space**

  In your design, white space is what allows you to breathe. When people use your design results, space gives them a place to breathe. The same goes for giving margins in the dashboard design. If there is not much space, the data may look cluttered and users may feel frustrated.

- **Color**

  Using effective color combinations can attract users' attention and communicate information more easily. Choose colors carefully to make your content easier to read. If you want the visual elements to stand out better than the background, try to maximize the contrast. It is recommended not to use gradients that have little contrast or are inefficient.

- **Number system**

  Excessive detail of a number makes it hard to read and hard to understand. If the number of digits is long, do not show all of them, but show approximate values. It is advisable to truncate unnecessary information. Make it easy for users to compare numbers.

- **Label**

  Use labels to convey the information quickly and efficiently you need. If the label is rotated, it is inconvenient for users to read. Even when using English abbreviations, use standard terms whenever possible.

Dashboards are intended to reduce the time and effort people spend understanding certain information by making it simpler to present complex and abstract data. Do not forget that the purpose of a dashboard is to communicate important information in a way people can understand. We need to be clear about what people need and express them nicely. The following sections will describe the quality dashboards of different industries.

3.4 HEALTHCARE QUALITY DASHBOARD

In the healthcare industry, medical appointment no-shows are important problems that critically affect the business. In order to reduce the number of patients no shows, it is essential to understand the potential factors causing the no-shows. This example dataset consists of 110,524 medical appointments and 14 related variables (https://www.kaggle.com/joniarroba/noshowappointments). The sample of this data set is shown in Table 3.1. This example focused on four key variables including gender, age, SMS (short message service) received, and no-show.

The main questions of this example are:

1. Does SMS help to reduce the number of patient no-shows?
2. Is the pattern of no-show different by age?
3. Is the characteristics of no show affected by gender?

This example aims to develop a dashboard to understand the patterns of no-shows by SMS, age, and gender. By applying the filtering of the appointment day, the dashboard will allow us to see the changes in no-show patterns over different days.

Before developing the dashboard, we need to construct an individual chart first. To answer the first question (Does SMS help to reduce the number of patient no-shows?), a horizontal bar chart may be considered.

Step 1: Open the data resource Excel file.
Step 2: Drag the "No-show" variable to the Rows on the shelf.
Step 3: Drag the "SMS received" variable to the Columns on the shelf. As a

---

TABLE 3.1
Sample Data Set of Medical Appointment No-shows

Gender	Age	SMS Received	No-show
F	62	0	No
M	56	0	No
F	62	0	No
F	8	0	No
F	56	0	No
F	76	0	No
F	23	0	Yes
F	39	0	Yes
F	21	0	No
F	19	0	No
F	30	0	No
M	29	1	Yes
F	22	0	No
M	28	0	No
F	54	0	No

Note: For SMS (short message service) received, 0 = no; 1 = yes

---

default setting, you may see the summation values of the "SMS received" variable.

Step 4: Under the "Show Me," select horizontal bars.

Step 5: Drag the "No-show" variable to the Color in Marks. This will differentiate the color between "No" and "Yes" for the "No-show" variable.

Step 6: Drag "Sum (SMS received)" measure to Label in Marks. This will visualize specific data values on top of the horizontal bar chart.

Step 7: By changing the name of Sheet 1 to "SMS Received Analysis for No Show," you may see the updated title on the horizontal bar chart (Figure 3.1).

We can now see that the patients who received SMS tended to have a lower number of no-shows than the patients who did not receive SMS. This indicates that SMS could be an effective reminder to reduce the number of patients no shows significantly.

The box plot may be considered to answer the second question (is the pattern of no-show different by age?).

Step 1: Create another sheet (Sheet 2) to construct a new chart.

Step 2: Drag "No-show" variable onto the Columns on the shelf.

FIGURE 3.1 The horizontal bar chart of SMS received by no-shows.

Step 3: Drag "Age" variable on the Rows on the shelf. You may see the Sum (Age) as a default value. Change this to Dimension to display all individual values in the data set.

Step 4: Under the "Show Me", select box-and-whisker plots.

Step 5: Drag "No-show" variable to the Color in Marks. This will differentiate the color between "No" and "Yes" for "No-show" variable.

Step 6: By changing the name of Sheet 2 to "Age Analysis for No Show," you may see the updated title on the vertical bar chart (Figure 3.2).

Based on the box plot, we can see no significant difference of age for medical appointment no show in terms of the median age and the variance (interquartile range). This indicates that there were no changes in behavior patterns by age.

To answer the last question (are the characteristics of no show affected by gender?), pie charts could be considered to visualize the portion of males and females for no shows.

Step 1: Create another sheet (Sheet 3) to construct a new chart.

Step 2: Drag "No-show" variable onto the Rows on the shelf.

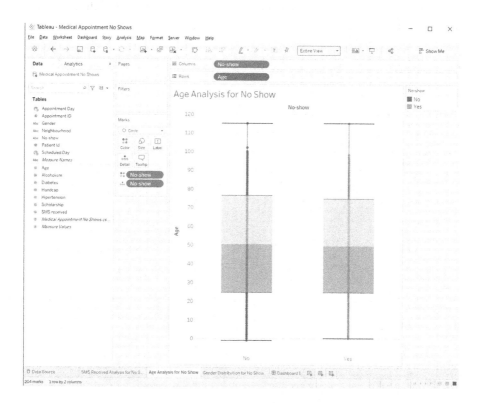

FIGURE 3.2   The box plot of the age difference for no-shows.

Step 3: Drag "Gender" variable to the Color in Marks. This will differentiate the color between F(females) and M(males).

Step 4: Under the dropdown menu of Marks, select "Pie" to conduct the pie chart. Otherwise, you could use "Show Me" guideline to choose Pie charts.

Step 5: By changing the name of Sheet 3 to "Gender Distribution for No Show", you may see the updated title on the pie charts (Figure 3.3).

Based on the pie chart, there was no significant difference in gender proportion for medical appointment no-shows. The proportion of males and females were balanced regardless of no-show events. This suggests that gender did not affect the patients' behavior patterns of medical appointment no-shows.

Now, it is time to construct a dashboard to combine all three charts together in one place.

Step 1: Create a new dashboard at the bottom panel.

Step 2: Under the Sheets, drag the "SMS Received Analysis" on the dashboard canvas. You could locate this horizontal bar plot on the top.

Step 3: Under the Sheets, drag the "Ange Analysis for No Show" on the dashboard canvas. You could locate this box plot on the bottom right.

Step 4: Under the Sheets, drag the "Gender Distribution for No Show" on the

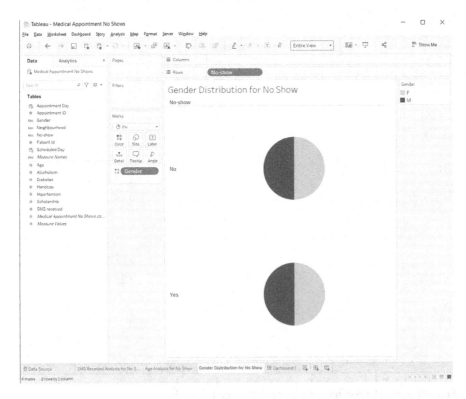

FIGURE 3.3   The pie charts of the gender proportion for no-shows.

dashboard canvas. You could locate this box plot on the bottom left.

Step 5: The legend of the Gender (F and M) would appear on the top right. Otherwise, you could drag and locate onto the top right (Figure 3.4).

Based on this dashboard, we could add the filtering function to interact with all three plots altogether.

Step 1: Go to "SMS Received Analysis for No Show" sheet.

Step 2: Drag "Appointment Day" to Filters on the shelf. You may see the pop-up box (Figure 3.5).

Step 3: We may select "Month / Day / Year" option for this example.

Step 4: You may see another pop-up box showing all the options of displaying Appointment Day. We can select "All" and hit OK (Figure 3.6).

Step 5: By clicking the "Show Filter" option, the filter could be displayed on the right panel (Figure 3.7).

Step 6: Change the display option to "Single Value (Slider)". You may see the slider display now (Figure 3.8).

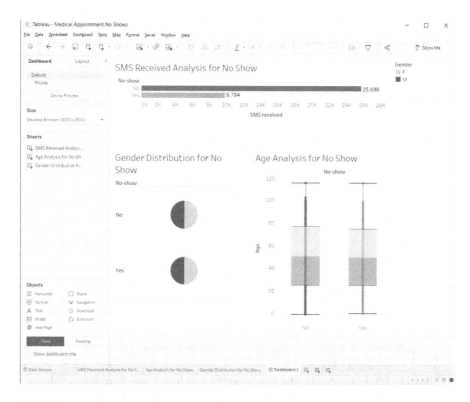

FIGURE 3.4 The dashboard of medical appointment no-shows.

FIGURE 3.5   Filter field options for "Appointment Day".

FIGURE 3.6   Filter options for "Appointment Day".

Step 7: Since we added a filter, it is time to apply this to the dashboard. Move to the dashboard sheet.

Step 8: If you right-click the mouse on the horizontal bar chart, select "Month, Day, Year of Appointment Day" under Filters. The filtering option would appear on the right side of the canvas (Figure 3.9).

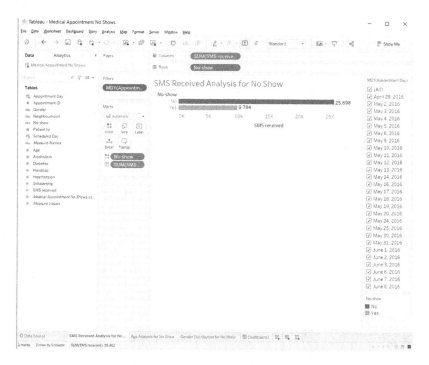

FIGURE 3.7 Filter of "Appointment Day" is displayed on the right panel.

FIGURE 3.8 Filter of "Appointment Day" is displayed as a slider on the right panel.

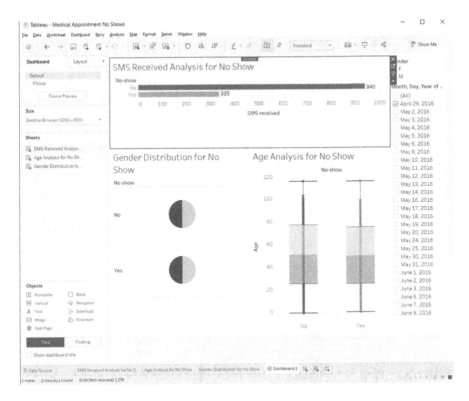

FIGURE 3.9   Filter of "Appointment Day" is displayed on the right panel.

Step 9: Change the display option to "Single Value (Slider)" and relocate the slide on the bottom of the canvas (Figure 3.10).

Step 10: Make sure to check if this filter is applied to the "All Using Related Data Sources" option under Apply to Worksheets. In that case, this filter would interact with all three plots displayed in the dashboard. By clicking the next button of the slider, we can see that the values of the horizontal bar chart are changed.

Step 11: Change the name of the dashboard to "Quality Analysis of Medical Appointment No Show". Check the box of "Show dashboard title" on the bottom left. You may see the final version of the dashboard (Figure 3.11).

Based on the dashboard, we can see that the SMS was the most critical factor affecting no-show occurrence. Other factors including gender and age did not show a big difference between no show and show. This dashboard result is based on aggregate measures of all appointment days. If we are interested in seeing the particular appointment day, we could adjust the slide bar, and we may encounter different trends of no show. This dashboard could be updated once we add more

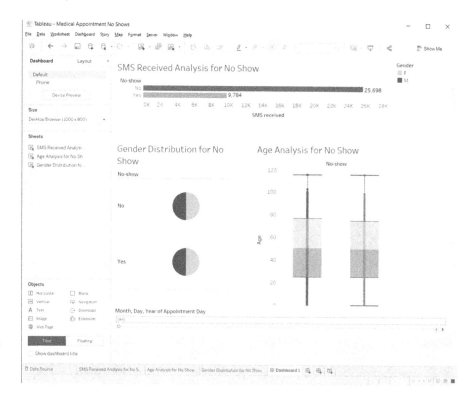

FIGURE 3.10   Filter of "Appointment Day" slider is displayed on the bottom of the canvas.

data in the original data resource Excel file. It will help the continuous monitoring of medical appointment no-show.

3.5   AIRLINE QUALITY DASHBOARD

Flight delay is a common issue and critically related to the airline business and passenger satisfaction. Many causes are affecting the flight delays including arrival and departure delays. The prevalence of flight delays is known to be different by airlines. It is important to understand the causes of flight delays to better control the flight schedule and improve passengers' service. This example dataset consists of 5,000 flight delays and related variables (https://www.kaggle.com/mrferozi/flight-delays), which was originally obtained from the US Department of Transport website. The sample of this data set is shown in Table 3.2. This example focused on four key variables including gender, age, SMS (short message service) received, and no-show.

The main questions of this example are:

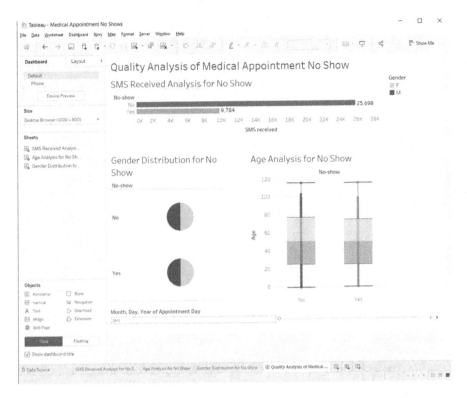

FIGURE 3.11   Final dashboard of quality analysis of medical appointment no show.

1. Are there differences in arrival and departure delays by origin airport?
2. What are the most common causes of flight delays?
3. Is there a relationship between arrival and departure delay?

This example aims to develop a dashboard that shows the characteristics of flight delays by origin airport, arrival delay, departure delay, and type of delays. The dashboard of flight delays could be useful to handle a large amount of data and see a variety of charts on one canvas. Filtering of the day can be added in the dashboard to see the changes in flight delays over a particular period of interest.

Before constructing the dashboard, we need to design and construct an individual chart first. To answer the first question (Are there a difference in arrival and departure delays by origin airport?), the vertical bar chart and line chart's dual combination may be considered.

    Step 1: Open the data resource Excel file.
    Step 2: Drag "DepDel15" variable to the Rows on the shelf. As a default setting, you may see the Sum (DepDel15) measure.
    Step 3: Drag "Origin Airport" variable to the Columns on the shelf.

TABLE 3.2
Sample Data Set of Flight Delays

Origin_Airport	Departure Delay	DepDel15	Arrival Delay	ArrDel15	Carrier Delay	Weather Delay
DFW	−5	0	−16	0	0	0
MSP	−4	0	−14	0	0	0
ATL	0	0	−12	0	0	0
MSP	1	0	−1	0	0	0
DEN	46	1	26	1	26	0
ATL	−3	0	−16	0	0	0
ATL	−4	0	−13	0	0	0
ATL	−2	0	−5	0	0	0
BOS	−6	0	−21	0	0	0
ATL	−5	0	−3	0	0	0
DTW	−9	0	−9	0	0	0
MCO	−1	0	−1	0	0	0
ATL	0	0	−7	0	0	0
LAS	−4	0	−17	0	0	0
MSP	−4	0	0	0	0	0

Note: DepDel15 = Departure delay more than 15 minutes; ArrDel15 = Arrival delay more than 15 minutes; 0 = no; 1 = yes

Step 4: For the drop-down menu in the Marks, select Bar shape.

Step 5: Drag "Sum (DepDel15)" measure to the Color in Marks. This will show the gradation of the color depending on the values of Sum (DepDel15). We can choose a preferred color option by clicking the Colors in Marks.

Step 6: On the toolbar, select the "Sorted descending" icon. This will help us to see the origin airport that caused the highest number of delays. The plot will be shown in Figure 3.12.

Step 7: Now, we can add another measure to develop a dual combination chart. Drag the "Arr Del morethan15" variable to the Rows on the shelf. As a default setting, you may see the Sum (Arr Del morethan15) measure.

Step 8: Select the "Dual Axis" setting on the pill of Sum(Arr Del morethan15).

Step 9: Select the "Synchronize Axis" setting on the right-hand side axis.

Step 10: Under the Marks of Sum (Arr Del morethan15), choose the Line shape. You may be able to see the dual combination chart (Figure 3.13).

Step 11: We can add a filtering function to interact with the plots in the dashboard later. Drag the "Day" variable on Filters on the shelf. You may see the pop-up box (Figure 3.14).

Step 12: We can hit OK to apply all ranges of values in the filter.

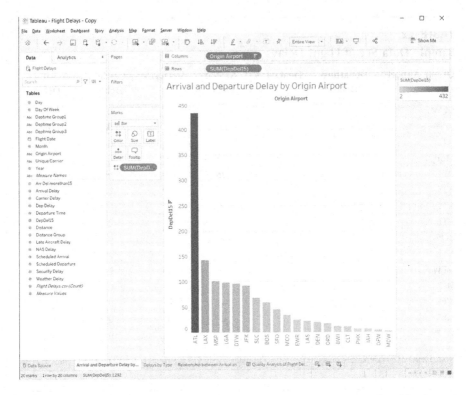

FIGURE 3.12   Vertical bar chart of summation of departure delays more than 15 minutes.

Step 13: Apply "Show Filter" options by right-clicking the Day pill.

Step 14: By changing the name of Sheet 1 to "Arrival and Departure Delay by Origin Airport", you may see the updated title on the chart (Figure 3.15).

Based on the chart, ATL airport showed the highest number of both arrival and departure delays. The overall trend of the arrival and departure delays were simar by origin airport. This suggests that the origin airport had an issue of the arrival delay tended to have the issue of the departure delay as well.

In order to answer the second question (What are the most common causes of flight delays?), a horizontal bar chart may be considered.

Step 1: Create another sheet (Sheet 2) to construct a new chart.

Step 2: Double click the "NAS Delay" variable. It will automatically show the summation values.

Step 3: Double click "Carrier Delay," "Late Aircraft Delay," "Weather Delay," and "Security Delay."

Step 4: Under the "Show Me," select horizontal bars.

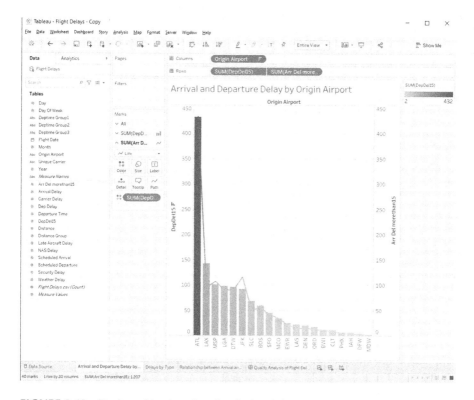

FIGURE 3.13   Dual combination plot of arrival and departure delay by origin airport.

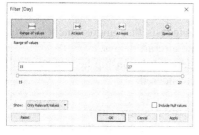

FIGURE 3.14   Pop-up box of filtering day.

Step 5: Drag the "Measure Names" variable to the Color in Marks. This will differentiate the color between Measure Names.

Step 6: Drag the "Measure Values" variable to the Label in Marks. This will show specific values of each measure on the horizontal bar chart.

Step 7: On the toolbar, select the "Sorted descending" icon.

Step 8: By changing the name of Sheet 2 to "Delays by Type," you may see the updated title on the horizontal bar chart (Figure 3.16).

Based on the horizontal bar chart, NAS (National Aviation System) delay was the most frequent issues followed by carrier delay and late aircraft delay. The security

FIGURE 3.15   The dual combination of the vertical bar and line charts of arrival and departure delay by origin airport.

delay was the least common occurrence. This suggests that improvement efforts could be prioritized on the NAS, carrier, and late aircraft delays.

In order to answer the second question (Is there a relationship between arrival and departure delay?), the scatter plot may be considered.

Step 1: Create another sheet (Sheet 3) to construct a new chart.

Step 2: Drag the "ArrivalDelay" variable to the Columns on the shelf. Select "Dimension" to display all individual values.

Step 3: Drag the "Dep Delay" variable to the Rows on the shelf. Select "Dimension" to display all individual values.

Step 4: For the drop-down menu in the Marks, select circle shape.

Step 5: Drag the "Origin Airport" variable to the Color in Marks. This will show different color codes by origin airports.

Step 6: By changing the name of Sheet 3 to "Relationship between Arrival and Departure Delay", you may see the updated title on the scatter plot (Figure 3.17).

FIGURE 3.16 Horizontal bar chart of delays by type.

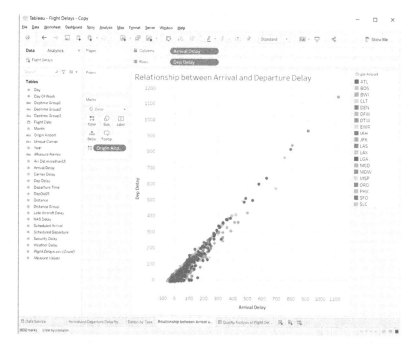

FIGURE 3.17 Scatter plot of arrival and departure delay.

Based on the scatter plot, there was a very clear linear relationship between arrival and departure delays. As the arrival delay time increased the departure delay time tended to increase as well. If we add trendlines on the scatter plot, we can see that the pattern was consistent regardless of different origin airports (Figure 3.18).

Now, we can develop a dashboard to compile the three charts mentioned above altogether.

Step 1: Create a new dashboard at the bottom panel.

Step 2: Under the Sheets, drag the "Arrival and Departure Delay by Origin Airport" on the dashboard canvas. You could locate this chart plot on the top left side.

Step 3: Under the Sheets, drag the "Relationship between Arrival and Departure Delay" on the dashboard canvas. You could locate this box plot on the top right.

Step 4: Under the Sheets, drag the "Delays by Type" on the dashboard canvas. You could locate this plot on the bottom.

Step 5: The legend of the color gradation of "DepDel15", color coding of "Origin Airport," and "Measure Names" would appear on the top right. Otherwise, you could drag and locate it onto the right-hand side of the canvas.

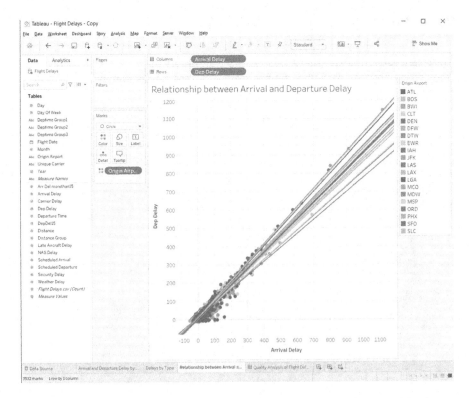

FIGURE 3.18 Scatter plot of arrival and departure delay with trend lines by origin airport.

Step 6: We could locate the filter of "Day" at the bottom of the canvas.

Step 7: Make sure to check if this filter is applied to the "All Using Related Data Sources" option under Apply to Worksheets.

Step 8: Change the name of the dashboard to "Quality Analysis of Flight Delays". Check the box of "Show dashboard title" on the bottom left. You may see the final version of the dashboard. By dragging the slide bar of the "Day" filter, you may see interactive changes of all three plots in the dashboard (Figure 3.19).

Based on the dashboard, the flight delays were significantly different by origin airport, and there was a different proportion of delay types. There was a clear positive linear relationship between arrival and departure delays. This finding is based on aggregate measures over all days collected in the data source. By adjusting the period of days, the results may be changed. This dashboard can be regular updated by adding new data in the data source Excel file.

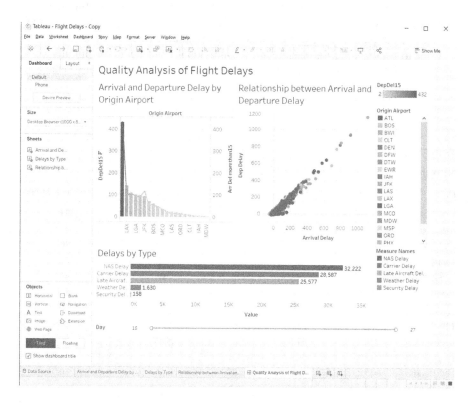

FIGURE 3.19   The final dashboard of quality analysis of flight delays.

3.6 MANUFACTURING QUALITY DASHBOARD

Machine failures have commonly occurred in the manufacturing process. These failures are critically affecting the productivity of the process. This example dataset consists of 142,193 cases of the machine failure records and related variables such as machine parameters and the environment characteristics (https://www.kaggle.com/binaicrai/machine-failure-data). The sample data set is shown in Table 3.3.

The main questions of this example are:

1. Is the number of machine failures changed over the years?
2. Is there a difference in temperature and leakage for machine failure?
3. Are parameter 1 speed and directory related to machine failure?

The purpose of this example is to understand the characteristics of machine failure by constructing a quality dashboard. The dashboard will help to understand the trend of failure over the years and determine the critical factors affecting the machine failure. The filtering of the year of data will be added to see interactive changes of the particular year's machine failure characteristics.

Prior to establishing the dashboard, an individual chart could be initially constructed. To answer the first question (Is the number of machine failures changed over the years?), the line chart could be used.

TABLE 3.3
Sample Data Set of Machine Failures

Date	Min_Temp	Max_Temp	Leakage	Parameter1_Dir	Parameter1_Speed
12/1/2008	13.4	22.9	0.6	W	44
12/2/2008	7.4	25.1	0	WNW	44
12/3/2008	12.9	25.7	0	WSW	46
12/4/2008	9.2	28	0	NE	24
12/5/2008	17.5	32.3	1	W	41
12/6/2008	14.6	29.7	0.2	WNW	56
12/7/2008	14.3	25	0	W	50
12/8/2008	7.7	26.7	0	W	35
12/9/2008	9.7	31.9	0	NNW	80
12/10/2008	13.1	30.1	1.4	W	28
12/11/2008	13.4	30.4	0	N	30
12/12/2008	15.9	21.7	2.2	NNE	31
12/13/2008	15.9	18.6	15.6	W	61
12/14/2008	12.6	21	3.6	SW	44
12/16/2008	9.8	27.7	NA	WNW	50

Step 1: Open the data resource Excel file.

Step 2: Drag the "Failure today" variable to the Rows on the shelf. Set Measure (count) for the variable.

Step 3: Drag the "Date" variable to the Columns on the shelf. As a default setting, it will show the Year (Date).

Step 4: For the drop-down menu in the Marks, select Line shape.

Step 5: By changing the name of Sheet 1 to "Number of Machine Failure by Year", you may see the updated title on the line chart (Figure 3.20).

Based on the line chart, the number of machine failures has been changed over the years. The number of machine failures has been generally increased from 2007 to 2016. Especially after 2008, there was a dramatic increase in the number of machine failures. After 2016, the number of machine failures was significantly reduced.

In order to answer the second question (Is there a difference in temperature and leakage for machine failure?), the horizontal bar charts may be considered.

Step 1: Create another sheet (Sheet 2) to construct a new chart.

Step 2: Drag the "Failure today" variable to the Rows on the shelf. Set "Dimension" setting.

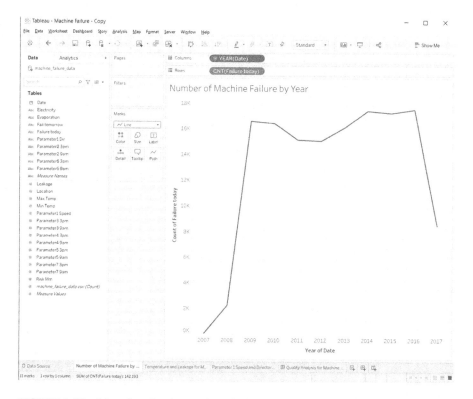

FIGURE 3.20   Line chart for the number of machine failures by year.

Step 3: Drag the "Max Temp" variable to the Columns on the shelf. Select the "Measure (Average)" setting to display the average values.

Step 4: Drag the "Min Temp" variable to the Columns on the shelf. Select the "Measure (Average)" setting.

Step 5: Drag the "Leakage" variable to the Columns on the shelf. Select the "Measure (Sum)" setting.

Step 6: Drag the "Failure today" variable to the Color in Marks. This will show different color codes by machine failure.

Step 7: By changing the name of Sheet 2 to "Temperature and Leakage for Machine Failure", you may see the updated title on the horizontal bar charts (Figure 3.21).

Based on the horizontal bar charts, leakage was highly related to machine failure. On the other hand, maximum and minimum temperatures were not significantly different with and without machine failure. It suggests that temperature may not be a critical factor affecting the machine failure. Inspection and maintenance of machines to minimize leakage would be an important practice to reduce machine failure.

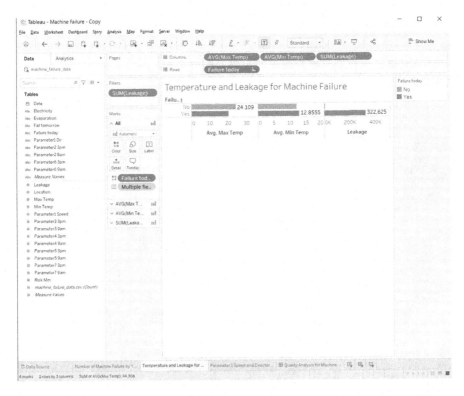

FIGURE 3.21   Horizontal bar charts for the temperature and leakage for machine failure.

In order to answer the third question (Are the parameter 1 speed and directory related to machine failure?), the pie charts may be considered.

Step 1: Create another sheet (Sheet 3) to construct a new chart.

Step 2: Drag the "Failure today" variable to the Columns on the shelf. Set "Dimension" setting.

Step 3: Under the drop-down menu for Marks, select the "Pie" shape.

Step 4: Drag the "Parameter1 Speed" variable to Angle under Marks. Select Measure (Average).

Step 5: Drag the "Parameter1 Speed" variable to Size under Marks. Select Measure (Average).

Step 6: Drag the "Parameter1 Dir" variable to the Color in Marks. This will show different color codes by Parameter1 directory.

Step 7: We can add a date filtering function to interact with the data over time. Drag the "Date" variable to the Filters on the shelf.

Step 8: Select "Show Filter" on the pill of the YEAR(Date) under Filters.

Step 9: Select the "Single Value (slider)" option for the display of the filter.

Step 10: By changing the name of Sheet 3 to "Parameter 1 Speed and Directory for Machine Failure", you may see the updated title on the pie charts (Figure 3.22).

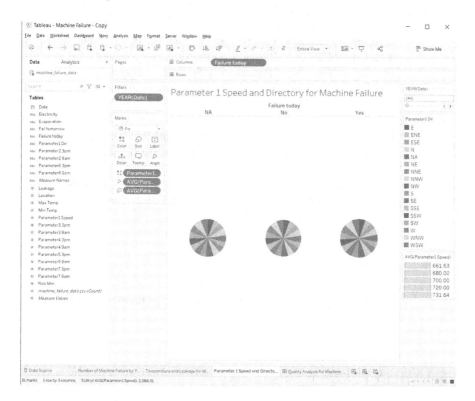

FIGURE 3.22 Pie charts for the parameter 1 speed and directory for machine failure.

Based on the pie charts, the average parameter 1 speed was slightly greater with the machine failure compared to the no machine failure case. There was no big difference in the parameter 1 speed by different directories. This suggests that parameter 1 speed and directory may not be critical factors affecting the machine failure.

We are ready to incorporate three charts into the dashboard.

Step 1: Create a new dashboard at the bottom panel.

Step 2: Under the Sheets, drag the "Number of Machine Failure by Year" on the dashboard canvas. You could locate this chart plot on the top.

Step 3: Under the Sheets, drag the "Temperature and Leakage for Machine Failure" on the dashboard canvas. You could locate this box plot at the center.

Step 4: Under the Sheets, drag the "Parameter 1 Speed and Directory for Machine Failure" on the dashboard canvas. You could locate this plot on the bottom.

Step 5: The legend of the "Failure today," "Parameter 1 Dir," "Avg. Parameter1 Speed" would appear on the top right. Otherwise, you could drag and locate it onto the right-hand side of the canvas.

Step 6: We could locate the filter of "Year of Date" onto the right-hand side of the canvas.

Step 7: Choose the "Selected Worksheets" option under Apply to Worksheets. You would encounter the pop-up box. Check "Temperature and Leakage for Machine Failure". Since "Number of Machine Failure by Year" shows the overall trend over the years, we may not need to apply filtering in this case. "Parameter 1 Speed and Directory for Machine Failure" was automatically checked since we build the filtering in this sheet (Figure 3.23).

Step 8: Change the name of the dashboard to "Quality Analysis of Machine Failure". Check the box of "Show dashboard title" on the bottom left. You may see the final version of the dashboard (Figure 3.24).

Based on the dashboard, machine failure has been changed over the years. Especially, there was a dramatic increase in machine failure from 2008 to 2009.

FIGURE 3.23   Apply filter to selected worksheets.

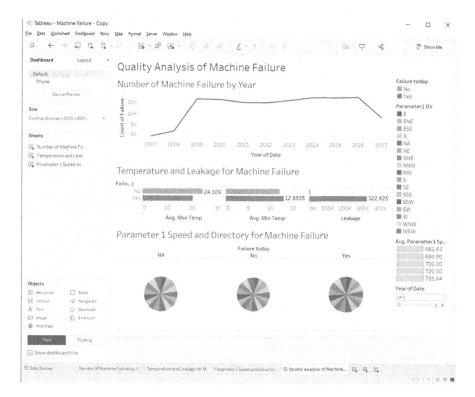

FIGURE 3.24   Final dashboard for the quality analysis of machine failure.

Based on the horizontal bar charts, leakage was the main issue related to machine failure whereas temperature was not significantly different between with and without machine failure condition. Based on pie charts, there was no big difference in parameter 1 speed and directory for machine failure. This dashboard could be regularly updated by adding new data into the data source Excel file. This dashboard will be helpful to have continuous monitoring of the process and control the quality level.

3.7   WAREHOUSE QUALITY DASHBOARD

Warehouse picking times are important factors affecting the quality and efficiency of logistics. If the picking times can be shortened without negatively affecting the quality of products, it could be directly related to cost savings, and increased customer satisfaction. The example dataset consists of 159,980 orders picked in the wholesale warehouse from 2015 to 2020 (https://www.kaggle.com/lewisgmorris/warehouse-picking-times). The sample data set is shown in Table 3.4. Here is the description of each variable:

PH_PICKEDB: Name of picker
PH_PICKSTA: Datetime of picking started

TABLE 3.4

Sample Data Set of Warehouse Picking Times

PH_PICKEDB	PH_PICKSTA	PH_PICKEND	PH_TOTALLI	PH_TOTALBO
PAUL	23/02/2015 12:25:47	23/02/2015 12:25:51	2	1
PAUL	23/02/2015 13:48:03	23/02/2015 13:48:05	1	1
PAUL	23/02/2015 14:18:13	23/02/2015 14:18:14	2	1
PAUL	23/02/2015 14:27:52	23/02/2015 14:29:55	2	1
LEWIS	26/02/2015 11:38:22	26/02/2015 11:39:27	3	1
LEWIS	26/02/2015 12:17:10	26/02/2015 12:18:06	2	1
LEWIS	3/3/2015 10:38	3/3/2015 10:39	2	1
LEWIS	3/3/2015 11:22	3/3/2015 11:23	2	1
LEWIS	3/3/2015 11:51	3/3/2015 11:52	2	1
PICKER	3/3/2015 12:21	3/3/2015 12:23	6	1
LEWIS	3/3/2015 12:41	3/3/2015 12:42	2	1
LEWIS	3/3/2015 12:55	3/3/2015 12:56	1	1
LEWIS	3/3/2015 15:22	3/3/2015 15:23	2	1
PICKER	3/3/2015 15:56	3/3/2015 15:56	4	0
LEWIS	3/3/2015 15:56	3/3/2015 15:57	2	1

PH_PICKEND: Datetime of picking ended
PH_TOTALLI: Number of total lines picked
PH_TOTALBO: Number of total boxes used

The main questions of this example are:

1. Is the number of total lines picked and total boxes used changed over the years?
2. What is the distribution of total boxes used by different pickers?
3. What is the trend of picking duration by different pickers?

This example aims to understand the characteristics of warehouse picking times by developing a quality dashboard. The interactive dashboard will help understand the trend of warehouse picking demand over the years and the distribution of picking workloads by different pickers. The filtering of picking year will be added to see the yearly changes of warehouse picking in the dashboard.

Before constructing the dashboard, individual charts will be initially constructed to answer the questions mentioned above. To answer the first question (Is the number of total lines picked and total boxes used changed over the years?), the vertical bar and line charts' dual combination could be used.

Step 1: Open the data resource Excel file.

Step 2: Drag the "Ph Pickend" variable to the Columns on the shelf. As a default setting, it will show the Year (Date).

Step 3: Drag the "Ph Totalbo" variable to the Columns on the shelf. As a default setting, it will show the SUM(Ph Totalbo). The line plot would be shown as an automatic setting.

Step 4: For the dropdown menu under Marks, set the "Bar" shape. The vertical box plot will be shown.

Step 5: Since the data includes the "Null" setting for the years, we could exclude this. Select "Filter" on the YEAR(Ph Picked) pill. Unmark the "Null" (Figure 3.25).

Step 6: You would be able to see the vertical bar chart between 2015 and 2020 (Figure 3.26).

Step 7: It is time to additional line plot on top of this vertical bar chart. Drag and drop the "Ph Totalli" variable right next to the SUM(Ph Totalbo) pill.

Step 8: For the dropdown menu under Marks, set "Line" shape. The line plot will be shown.

Step 9: Set "Dual Axis" on the axis of "Ph Totalli" variable.

Step 10: By changing the name of Sheet 1 to "Total Lines and Boxes Picked over Time", you may see the updated title on the chart (Figure 3.27).

Based on the combination of the vertical bar and line charts, there were changes in the total boxes used and total lines picked over the years. These two variables (total boxes used and total lines picked) showed a similar trend over time. There was a dramatic increase in the demand from 2015 to 2016. Although there was a dramatic

FIGURE 3.25 Filter options of "Year of Ph Pickend".

FIGURE 3.26 Step 6 for creating the combination of the vertical bar and line charts.

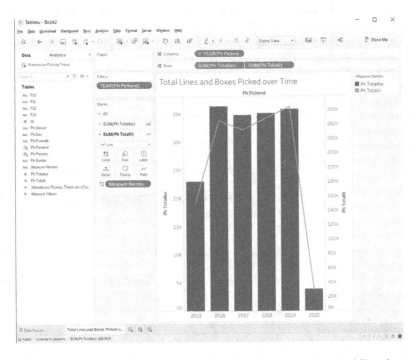

FIGURE 3.27 Step 10 for creating the combination of the vertical bar and line charts.

decrease from 2019 to 2020, this could be partially due to insufficient data collected in 2020.

In order to answer the second question (What is the distribution of total boxes used by different pickers?), the pie chart may be considered.

Step 1: Create another sheet (Sheet 2) to construct a new chart.

Step 2: Select "Pie" shape under Marks.

Step 3: Drag and drop the "Ph Pickedb" variable to Color under Marks. Set the Pie chart as "Entire View".

Step 4: Drag and drop the "Ph Totalbo" variable to Angle under Marks. You may be able to see the pie chart as seen below (Figure 3.28).

Step 5: We can add labels on the pie chart as well. Drag and drop the "Ph Pickedb" variable to Label under Marks.

Step 6: Drag and drop the "Ph Totalbo" variable to Label under Marks. To label the proportion of variable, select "Percent of Total" under Quick Table Calculation (Figure 3.29).

Step 7: You may be able to see the pie chart with updated labels (Figure 3.30).

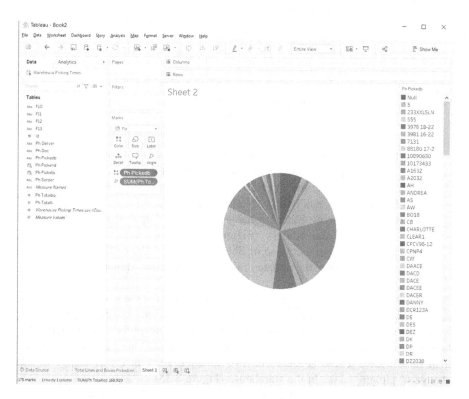

FIGURE 3.28 Step 4 for creating the pie chart.

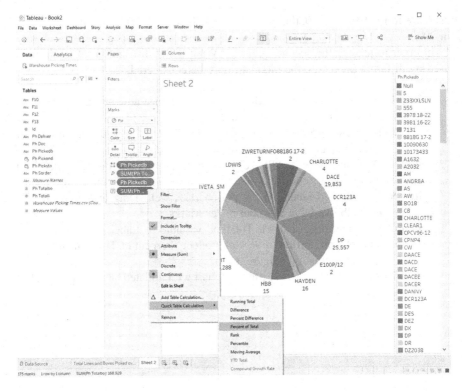

FIGURE 3.29   Step 6 for creating the pie chart.

Step 8: We can add filtering of the "Ph Pickend" variable to see the changes of the variable over the years. Drag and drop the "Ph Pickend" variable to Filters. Select the "Years" option (Figure 3.31).

Step 9: Select all years except "Null" (Figure 3.32).

Step 10: Select "Show Filter." Change the display option of the filtering to "Single Value (slider)" (Figure 3.33).

Step 11: By changing the name of Sheet 2 to "Total Boxes Used by Pickers," you may see the updated title on the pie chart (Figure 3.34).

Based on the pie chart, there was a different workload for the total boxes used by pickers. Picker name "IT" used the highest number of total boxes over the years, which indicated the highest workload followed by the picker name "DP." By looking at the recent year "2019", both pickers IT and DP used about 66% of the total boxes used. These suggest that two to three workers are primarily in the change of picking boxes in the warehouse (Figure 3.35).

In order to answer the third question (What is the trend of picking duration by different pickers?), the Pareto chart may be considered.

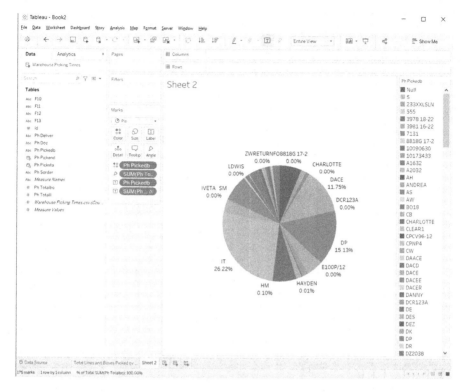

FIGURE 3.30   Step 7 for creating the pie chart.

FIGURE 3.31   Step 8 for creating the pie chart.

FIGURE 3.32   Step 9 for creating the pie chart.

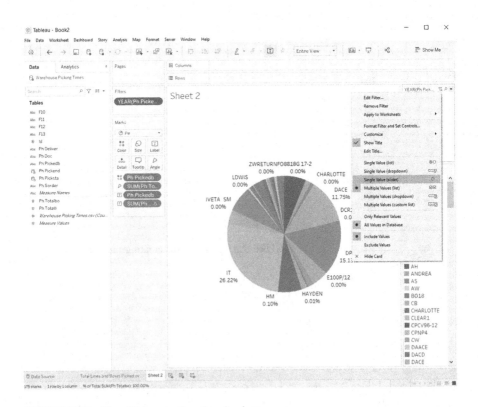

FIGURE 3.33   Step 10 for creating the pie chart.

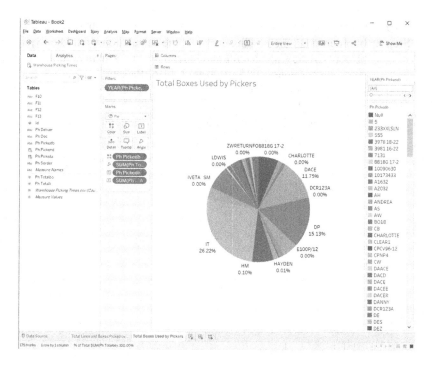

FIGURE 3.34 Step 11 for creating the pie chart.

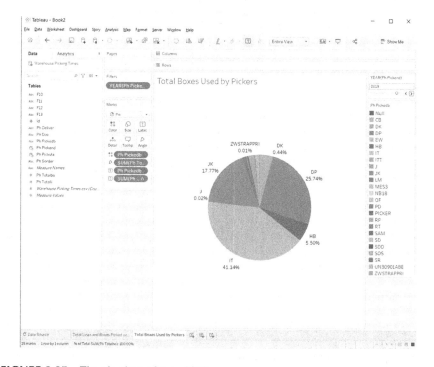

FIGURE 3.35 The pie chart of year 2019.

Step 1: Create another sheet (Sheet 3) to construct a new chart.

Step 2: In order to get the picking duration, the calculation would be required. Select "Create Calculated Field." Set name as "Picking Duration" and write the formula as "[Ph Pickend] – [Ph Picksta]" (Figure 3.36).

Step 3: Drag and drop the "Picking Duration" variable to Rows. As a default setting, SUM(Picking Duration) will be set.

Step 4: Drag and drop the "Ph Pickedb" variable to Columns. You may see the vertical bar chart with many categories (Figure 3.37).

FIGURE 3.36   Step 2 for creating the Pareto chart.

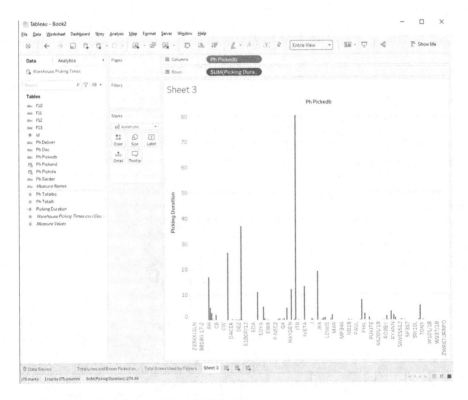

FIGURE 3.37   Step 4 for creating the Pareto chart.

Step 5: We could only show the top 10 pickers. Select "Filter" on the "Ph Pickedb" pill. On the "Top" tab, select "By field" and set the value as 10. Hit OK (Figure 3.38).

Step 6: You may be able to see the top 10 pickers. We can sort the values by clicking the "sorted descending" icon in the toolbar (Figure 3.39).

Step 7: Drag and drop the "Picking Duation" variable to Colors under Marks. This will show the colors gradation based on the amount of picking duration (Figure 3.40).

Step 8: Now, we can add an additional line chart to show the cumulative percentage of picking duration. Drag and drop the "Picking duration" variable to Rows right next to the existing pill. Set "Line" shape under Marks. Remove color setting under Marks. Set "orange" colors for the line (Figure 3.41).

Step 9: This line plot still shows the picking duration. To see cumulative percentage values, select "Add Table Calculation" (Figure 3.42).

Step 10: Set "Running Total" as the Primary Calculation Type. Check the box of "Add secondary calculation." For the Secondary Calculation Type, set "Percent of Total" (Figure 3.43).

Step 11: Set "Dual Axis" on the second pill in Rows (Figure 3.44).

Step 12: We can also add labels on both vertical bar and line charts. Drag and drop the "SUM(Picking Duration)" variable to Label under the first Marks. Drag and drop "SUM(Picking Duration) Table calculation" to Label under the second Marks.

FIGURE 3.38   Step 5 for creating the Pareto chart.

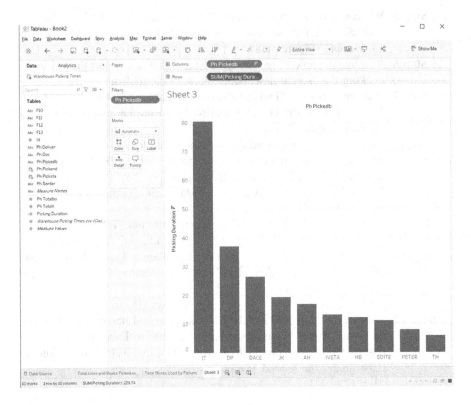

FIGURE 3.39   Step 6 for creating the Pareto chart.

Step 13: By changing the name of Sheet 3 to "Picking Duration by Pickers," you may see the updated title on the Pareto chart (Figure 3.45).

Step 14: Based on the Pareto chart's 80-20 rule, we can add the 80% reference line on the chart. Select "Add Reference Line" on the second y-axis. Select "Entire Table" and "Constant". Write a value of 0.8 (Figure 3.46).

Step 15: Final version of the Pareto chart would be shown (Figure 3.47).

Based on the Pareto chart, we can see that picking duration was the highest with the picker "IT" followed by "DP." The majority (over 80%) of picking duration was accounted for by six pickers in this warehouse. This suggests that there was a concentrated work demand on several pickers.

FIGURE 3.40 Step 7 for creating the Pareto chart.

Since three charts were constructed, we can build the dashboard.

Step 1: Create a new dashboard at the bottom panel.

Step 2: Under the Sheets, drag the "Picking Duration by Pickers" on the dashboard canvas.

Step 3: Under the Sheets, drag the "Total Lines and Boxes Picked over Time" on the dashboard canvas. You could locate this box plot on the bottom.

Step 4: Under the Sheets, drag the "Total Boxed Used by Pickers" on the dashboard canvas. You could locate this plot on the right bottom. We can slightly adjust the size of each plot for better visualization.

Step 5: We could apply the filtering of the "Year" option to selected plots. Select "Selected Worksheets" under Apply to Worksheets (Figure 3.48).

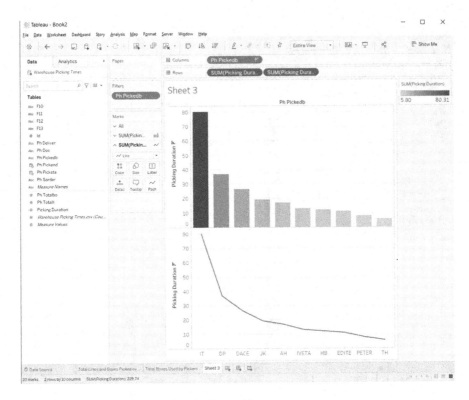

FIGURE 3.41 Step 8 for creating the Pareto chart.

Step 6: In the pop-up box, select the "Picking Duration by Picker" sheet. Since "Total Lines and Boxed Picked over the years" do not need filtering of years, we could exclude that (Figure 3.49).

Step 7: Change the name of the dashboard to "Quality Analysis of Warehouse Picking Times". Check the box of "Show dashboard title" on the bottom left. You may see the final version of the dashboard (Figure 3.50).

Based on the final dashboard, we can see the overall trend of warehouse picking times over the years and by different pickers. The demand for warehouse picking has been dramatically increasing from 2015 to 2016, and there was a steady demand from 2016 to 2019. Data on warehousing picking in 2020 is still in an ongoing process. As seen

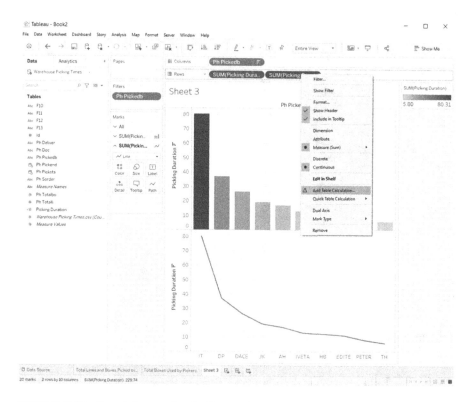

FIGURE 3.42 Step 9 for creating the Pareto chart.

FIGURE 3.43 Step 10 for creating the Pareto chart.

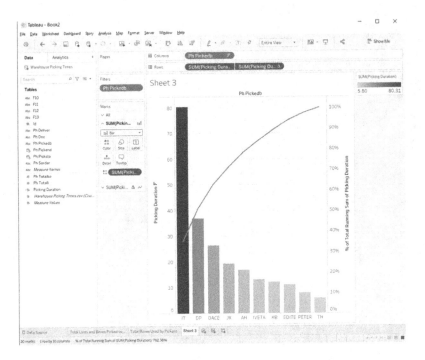

FIGURE 3.44 Step 11 for creating the Pareto chart.

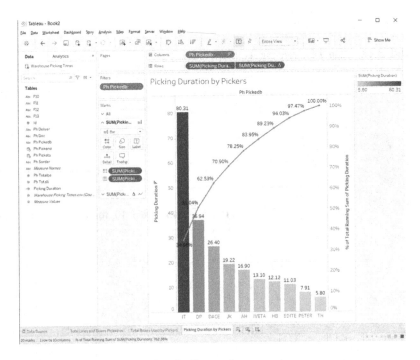

FIGURE 3.45 Step 13 for creating the Pareto chart.

FIGURE 3.46   Step 14 for creating the Pareto chart.

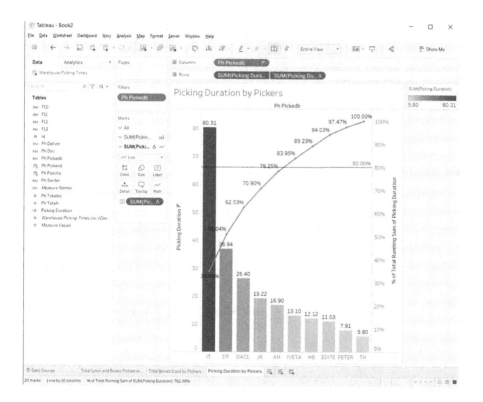

FIGURE 3.47   Step 15 for creating the Pareto chart.

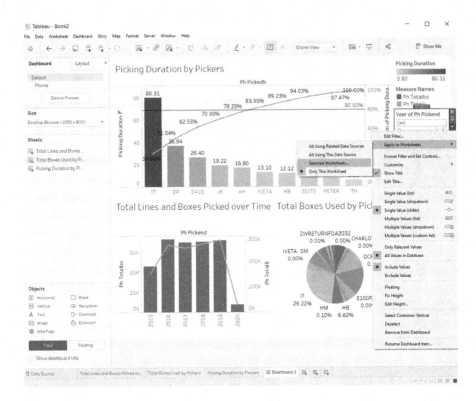

FIGURE 3.48   Step 5 for creating the dashboard.

FIGURE 3.49   Step 6 for creating the dashboard.

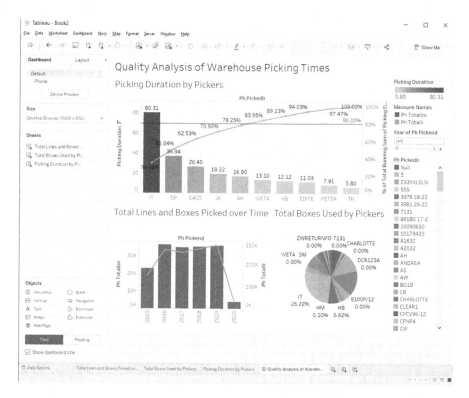

FIGURE 3.50 Step 7 for creating the dashboard.

in the Pareto and pie charts, several pickers were in charge of most of the warehouse picking demands. If we see the warehouse picking times of the year 2019 by adjusting the slide bar in the dashboard, three pickers (IT, DP, and JK) take charge of greater than 90% of the picking workload. This dashboard would be continuously updated once new data is added to the data source Excel file. It can also be shared by all stakeholders including pickers, staff, managers, supervisors, heads, and quality engineers to communicate for the quality improvements effectively (Figure 3.51).

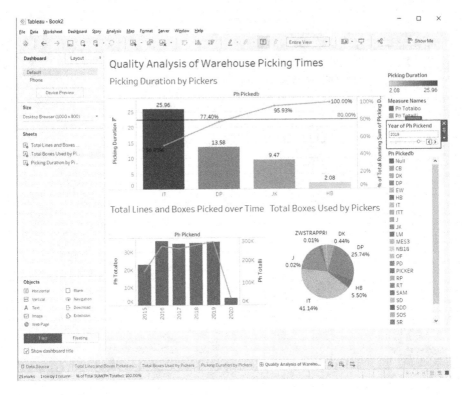

FIGURE 3.51   The dashboard of the year 2019.

4 Case Studies

CHAPTER OVERVIEW AND EXPECTED LEARNING OUTCOMES

In this chapter, we will introduce the concepts of case studies and data storytelling. We will discuss effective data storytelling strategies and introduce six different case studies. Examples of quality analysis charts and dashboards will be provided to answer the main questions under each case study. After gaining insights from each dataset, we will discuss practical implications and quality improvement suggestions.

After studying this chapter, expected learning outcomes are:

1. Explain the concepts of case studies and data storytelling.
2. Explain the strategies of compelling data storytelling.
3. Know how to use Tableau to construct quality analysis charts and dashboards.
4. Interpret the charts and dashboard and provide effective quality improvement suggestions.

4.1 CASE STUDIES AND DATA STORYTELLING

Case studies are not a way of finding out the factors influencing an outcome in a controlled situation. In other words, rather than collecting data for specific people within the laboratory, it is a kind of analysis method by collecting and analyzing data based on the "similarity" occurring in various industries or society with a broader perspective. Case studies need to be applied to solve difficult variables, or various problems that are suspicious and are not resolved. For example, if you want to practice analyzing the causes and finding solutions to the issues that may occur on a daily basis, such as a sharp increase in defect rates, a sharp drop in service quality and satisfaction, and a surge in production costs, case studies are effective. The critical point in the case study comes from constant inquiry, problem consciousness, and a desire to achieve the solution.

The cases covered in this chapter will be suitable for these exercises and are practical cases that you may encounter in academic or industrial institutions. After collecting and analyzing data, finding problems, and suggesting solutions, what should be next? It is communication. Through communication, problems and solutions should be shared with stakeholders, and actions must be taken to the next step. If you use storytelling techniques, you can communicate effectively.

We can leverage compelling storytelling to achieve our goal via data analytics, charts, and dashboard created by Tableau. Before jumping into a case study, we will learn techniques for compelling storytelling. Let us make a GAME plan that is widely known and easy to use in communication. GAME is an acronym for Goal, Audience, Message, and Engagement.

4.1.1 GOAL

We need to determine what we are looking to achieve with our story, and it should be as concrete as possible. Are you trying to make someone take action? For example, are you looking to get funding for investment or taking steps for improvement? Are we encouraging to get support from management? Regardless of our goal, make sure we can determine when that goal has been reached.

4.1.2 AUDIENCE

We should figure out who our audience is. Who is the decision-maker? Who can affect our end goal, and Who can influence the process? We should determine who our audience is and how they want data presented to deliver their decision.

4.1.3 MESSAGE

We should figure out the most important message to get across to your audience. We can narrow down our statement to 1–3 key points (single sentences) that we want our audience to deliver.

4.1.4 ENGAGEMENT

After determining the goal, audience, and message, we need to determine the best way to engage with our audience. This includes selecting a channel and medium for goal, audience, and message. Examples of channels are email, website, social media, or webinars, or even in-person presentations.

4.2 RED WINE QUALITY (CASE 1)

4.2.1 INTRODUCTION OF DATASET

The wine quality is an essential factor for wine collectors and wine sellers. In general, complexity, balance, typicity, intensity, and finish are key indicators of wine quality. This wine quality is known to be affected by climate, weather, temperature, sunlight, growing practices, and winemaking practices. These factors could result in a varied range of wine quality.

A dataset consists of several physicochemical properties of the wine and subjective rating of the wine quality (between 0 and 10) (Cortez, Cerdeira, Almeida, Matos, & Reis, 2009). The data set includes 1,599 red wines' 11 different physicochemical properties and their quality ratings. The description of each measure is shown in Table 4.1.

We could determine the relationship between the wine's physicochemical properties and quality ratings based on this data. This understanding would help to understand critical factors to improve wine quality.

TABLE 4.1
The Description of Physiochemical Properties and the Quality Rating

Variable	Description
Fixed acidity	Higher value indicates wine tastes sour
Volatile acidity	Low value is related to fruity-smelling
Citric acid	Greater value increases the sour taste
Residual sugar	Increased sugar indicates more sweetness
Chlorides	The amount of salt in the wine
Free sulfur dioxide	Lower value is related to wines with more color
Total sulfur dioxide	Protects the wine from oxidation
Density	Lower density is related to increased alcohol level
pH	Higher pH gives brighter ruby color to the wine
Sulphates	It helps to preserve the wine
Alcohol	It adds viscosity and balances sweetness and acidity
Quality	It was determined from sensory data (0: lowest quality; 10: highest quality)

Questions

- What is the distribution of wine quality?
- Is there a relationship between the properties and wine quality?
- What are the differences of variations in properties between low- and high-quality wine?
- What is the good combination of multiple properties producing a good quality wine?

The full data set is available in Kaggle (https://www.kaggle.com/uciml/red-wine-quality-cortez-et-al-2009). Table 4.2 shows the example of the partial data set including only 4 properties and the quality rating.

4.2.2 TABLEAU EXAMPLE

The histogram was constructed to see the distribution of red wine quality ratings to address the first question (what is the distribution of wine quality?). As seen in Figure 4.1, most of the red wines' quality was between 5 and 7. There were few exceptionally bad wines (below quality 4) and excellent wines (above quality 8). This suggests that most red wines' quality levels were in the mid-range.

To answer the second question (is there a relationship between the properties and wine quality?), the scatterplot was created to see the relationship between individual property and the quality rating. A possible of 11 scatter plots could be constructed to diagnose the relationship between individual property and wine quality. Only scatter plots showing the meaningful trends were introduced here. Figure 4.2 shows the example of the scatterplot between volatile acidity and wine quality. There was a negative linear relationship between the volatile acidity and the quality. In other

TABLE 4.2

Example Data of Wine Properties and Quality Rating

Fixed Acidity	Volatile Acidity	Citric Acid	Residual Sugar	Quality
7.4	0.7	0	1.9	5
7.8	0.88	0	2.6	5
7.8	0.76	0.04	2.3	5
11.2	0.28	0.56	1.9	6
7.4	0.7	0	1.9	5
7.4	0.66	0	1.8	5
7.9	0.6	0.06	1.6	5
7.3	0.65	0	1.2	7
7.8	0.58	0.02	2	7
7.5	0.5	0.36	6.1	5

words, the quality of wine was increased as the volatile acidity was lowered. Peopled tended to rate higher quality scores for the wines with more fruity-smelling than those with a more sharp smell.

Another meaningful scatter plot was constructed for the data pair of the alcohol content and the wine quality as seen in Figure 4.3. Higher quality wines tended to have greater alcohol content. It is known that the proper amount of alcohol content helps to balance the sweetness and acidity of the wine. This indicates that alcohol content is one of the critical factors affecting wine quality.

To answer the third question (what are differences of variations in properties between low- and high-quality wine?), the box plot was constructed to compare the variability of volatile acidity across different wine quality ratings, as seen in Figure 4.4. It showed that the highest quality wines (rating 8) had the lowest variability of volatile acidity whereas the lowest quality wines (rating 3) had the highest variability of volatile acidity. This suggests that high-quality wines tended to have a consistent range of volatile acidity.

To answer the last question (what are the good combination of multiple properties producing a good quality wine?), the scatter plot with the color option was constructed to understand the relationship between three variables including the alcohol content, volatile acidity, and wine quality as seen in Figure 4.5. Two reference lines were added for the average values of the alcohol content and volatile acidity. This showed a clear trend that high-quality wines were mostly grouped with the combination of high alcohol (greater than the average of 10.5%) and low volatile acidity (lower than the average of 0.53). It means that people preferred wine with fruity-smell and high alcohol content.

We could have a closer look at the three-way relationship of the alcohol content, volatile acidity, and wine quality as seen in Figure 4.6. As the wine quality increased, more data points were located at the combination of high alcohol and low volatile acidity. For the lowest quality wine (quality score of 3), none of the wines belonged to the combination of high alcohol and low volatile acidity.

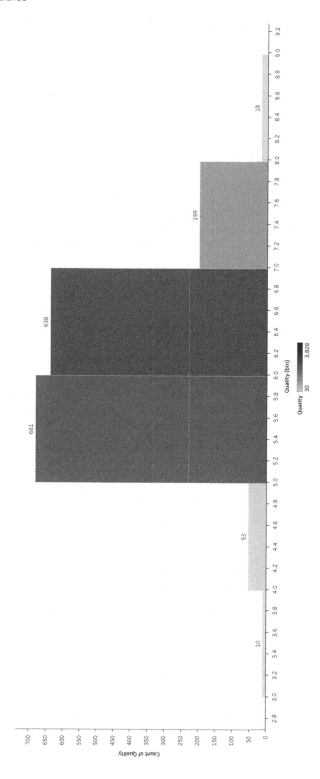

FIGURE 4.1 The histogram of wine quality.

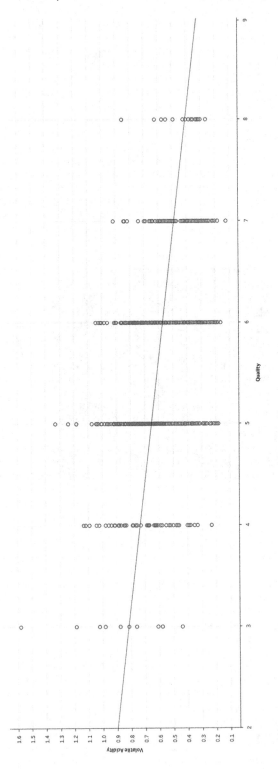

FIGURE 4.2   The scatter plot of the volatile acidity and wine quality.

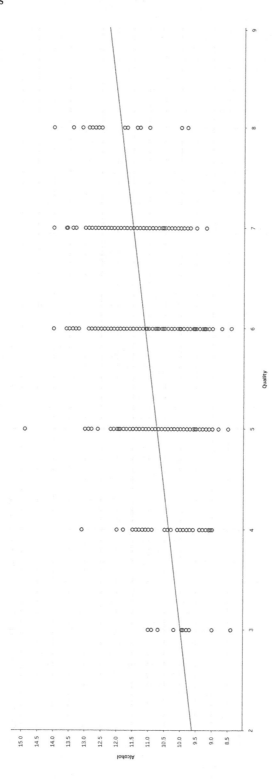

FIGURE 4.3 The scatterplot of alcohol content and wine quality.

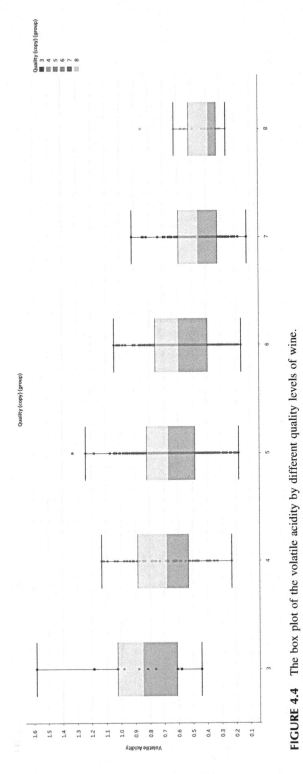

FIGURE 4.4 The box plot of the volatile acidity by different quality levels of wine.

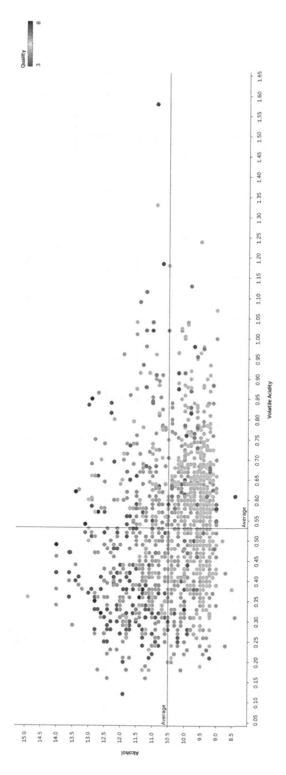

FIGURE 4.5 The scatter plot of the alcohol content and volatile acidity. The wine's quality levels were colored (low quality: red; high quality: blue).

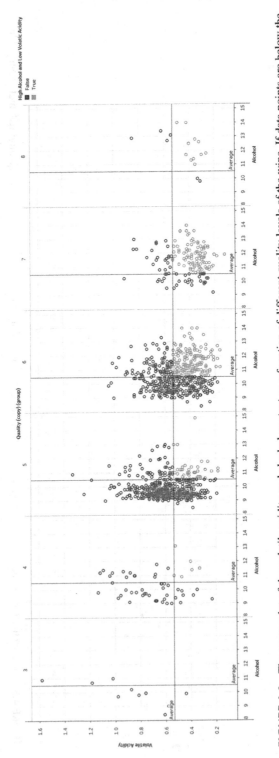

FIGURE 4.6 The scatterplot of the volatile acidity and alcohol content as a function of different quality levels of the wine. If data points are below the average of volatile acidity, and above the average of alcohol content, the orange color was coded.

To summarize some key findings, the dashboard, including histogram, box plot, and scatter plot, was created in Figure 4.7. In summary, most wines were rated at the mid-range quality (5–7). There were few poor or exceptional quality wines. High-quality wines tended to have a low variability of volatile acidity compared to lower-quality wines. As the wine quality increased, there was an increased amount of low volatile acidity, and high alcohol content.

The volatile acidity is known as an important factor to give the aromas of the wine. If the amount of volatile acidity is high, it could cause a too strong smell, and ruin the balance. The clean winemaking process is an essential factor in the low amount of volatile acidity of wines. These facts are well aligned with our findings. This could be an important consideration for the wine producers to improve the winemaking process and wine quality. For wine collectors or sellers, the wine showing an aroma could be an important factor affecting the subjective wine quality.

TABLEAU DASHBOARD AND DATA STORYTELLING

GOAL

This dashboard makes it easy for those involved in winemaking and sales to understand which factors significantly impact wine quality and consumer satisfaction.

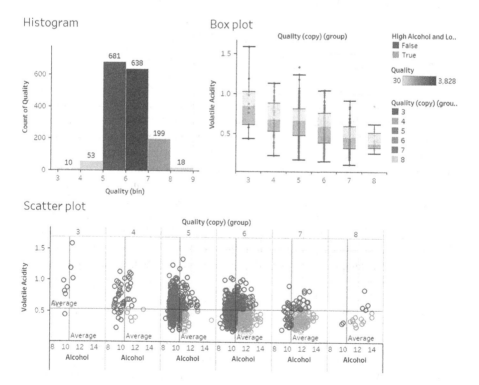

FIGURE 4.7   The dashboard of the histogram, box plot and scatter plot.

AUDIENCE

This dashboard's primary audience is wine business stakeholders, winemakers, wine sellers, and wine quality analysts.

MESSAGE

Through the dashboard, we can get answers to the following questions.

- What is the distribution of wine quality that consumers feel?
- What components of wine have a close influence on the quality of wine?
- Is there a clear difference in wine composition between good and bad wines?

The dashboard allows stakeholders to discuss these questions and take action to improve quality.

ENGAGEMENT

The dashboard developed can be updated daily on the screen of the winemaking site. Wine business representatives can check the status of wine quality on a personal computer through a network connection in the office.

4.3 AIRLINE PASSENGER SATISFACTION (CASE 2)

4.3.1 INTRODUCTION OF DATASET

Airline success is critically related to the satisfaction of airline passengers. Airlines frequently conduct a survey study to understand customers' perspectives. It is known that many factors are affecting airline customer experience. Some factors include flight schedule options, ease of reservations, check-in process, boarding process, on-time arrival, baggage handling, and etc. It is crucial to determine which factor is a key differentiator for high-quality service of airlines.

The example data set includes the data from an airline passenger satisfaction survey (adapted from https://www.kaggle.com/teejmahal20/airline-passenger-satisfaction). This data consists of 103,904 airline passengers' responses, and their associated airline factors were collected as well. A total of 23 variables were collected. Table 4.3 describes the example of several variables considered in this data set.

Based on this data, we could identify the key factors affecting the satisfaction of airline passengers.

Questions

- Which factor is a differentiator for the high satisfaction of the airline service?
- Is there a difference in the satisfaction between loyal and disloyal passengers?
- Does airline class (Business, Eco, Eco Plus) affect passenger satisfaction?
- Do arrival and departure delays affect passenger satisfaction?

TABLE 4.3
The Example of Factors and their Description

Variable	Description
Gender	Male, Female
Customer type	Loyal, disloyal customers
Type of travel	Personal, business travel
Class	Business, Eco, Eco Plus
Age	Age of the passengers
Inflight entertainment	Satisfaction level of inflight entertainment (0: not applicable, 1 to 5)
Inflight wifi	Satisfaction level of inflight entertainment (0: not applicable, 1 to 5)
Online boarding	Satisfaction of online boarding (0: not applicable, 1 to 5)
Satisfaction	Airline satisfaction level (satisfaction, neutral/dissatisfaction)

The full data set could be accessed in Kaggle (https://www.kaggle.com/teejmahal20/airline-passenger-satisfaction). Table 4.4 shows the example of the partial data set of the survey results related to airline passenger satisfaction.

4.3.2 TABLEAU EXAMPLE

To address the first question (which factor is a differentiator for the airline service's high satisfaction), side-by-side bars were constructed for the multiple measures. Figure 4.8 shows the percentage difference of satisfaction of multiple measures (online boarding, inflight entertainment, inflight wifi, seat comfort, legroom service, onboard service, cleanliness, check-in service, food and drink, ease of online booking, and inflight service) between satisfied and neutral/dissatisfied customers.

TABLE 4.4
Partial Data Set of the Survey Results Regarding Airline Passenger Satisfaction

Gender	Customer Type	Age	Type of Travel	Class	Inflight Wifi
Male	Loyal Customer	13	Personal Travel	Eco Plus	3
Male	Disloyal Customer	25	Business Travel	Business	3
Female	Loyal Customer	26	Business Travel	Business	2
Female	Loyal Customer	25	Business Travel	Business	2
Male	Loyal Customer	61	Business Travel	Business	3
Female	Loyal Customer	26	Personal Travel	Eco	3
Male	Loyal Customer	47	Personal Travel	Eco	2
Female	Loyal Customer	52	Business Travel	Business	4
Female	Loyal Customer	41	Business Travel	Business	1
Male	Disloyal Customer	20	Business Travel	Eco	3

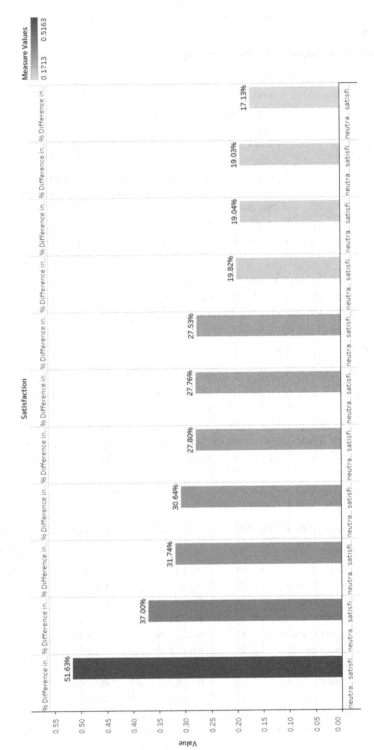

FIGURE 4.8 Bar charts of multiple satisfaction measures (percentage difference between satisfied and neutral/dissatisfied customers).

The percentage difference values were sorted from the highest value to the lowest value. This indicates that the online boarding experience was the most important factor affecting the overall satisfaction of airline service. With the online boarding process, passengers do not have to stand in line, and quickly pass the required formalities to receive the boarding passes. This convenient and efficient process was considered as the most important factor affecting overall satisfaction. In addition, inflight entertainment, inflight wifi, and seat comfort were also found as critical factors affecting the overall satisfaction levels. Airlines' entertainment/wifi service is an essential element of a passengers' onboard experience. The wifi service enables passengers to access live TV, messaging service, radio, and digital streaming service of music and podcasts. Customers have a more enjoyable onboard experience with the entertainment/wifi service's aid, they were more satisfied with the overall airline service.

To address the second question (is there a difference in the satisfaction between loyal and disloyal passengers?), the side-by-side bars were constructed as seen in Figure 4.9. Loyal customers tended to have a higher satisfaction of the online boarding, seat comfort, inflight entertainment, cleanliness, food and drink, check-in service, and ease of online booking than disloyal customers. This difference could be related to the benefit that airlines offered to loyal customers. Many airlines offer premium check-in such as early access to better seats (e.g., exit row seats) at no cost to loyal customers during the online boarding process, which could increase satisfaction compared to disloyal customers. In addition, many airlines offer free access to inflight entertainment to loyal customers using passengers' personal electronic devices, which could raise the satisfaction of the onboard experience.

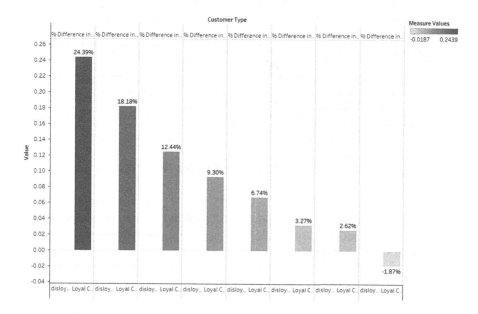

FIGURE 4.9 Bar charts of multiple satisfaction measures (percentage difference between loyal and disloyal customers).

For the third question (does airline class (Business, Eco, Eco Plus) affect passenger satisfaction?), another side-by-side bar could be constructed to compare the airline class measures. Figure 4.10 shows that the business class tended to have greater satisfaction with online boarding, seat comfort, inflight entertainment, check-in service, cleanliness, ease of online booking, inflight service, and food and drink compared to other classes. One of the business class's well-known benefits includes the high quality of seating, food, and drink, which were well aligned with the results in Figure 4.10. As expected, the premium Business class has access to a variety of entertainment programs including movies, radio, TV, and game, and some airlines provide noise-canceling headphones to improve the sound quality. Interestingly, there was no big increase (less than 3%) of satisfaction between the Eco and Eco Plus classes of most measures. This suggests that if Eco Plus requires more cost than Eco, Eco Plus may not be a good option.

The dashboard was created to include both bar charts and the scatter plot to address the last question (do arrival and departure delay affect passenger satisfaction?) as seen in Figure 4.11. The bar chart showed that there was a significant increase (31–36%) of both arrival and departure delays among the neutral/dissatisfied customers compared to satisfied customers. The scatter plot showed that there was a positive linear relationship between the arrival delay and departure delay. It means that as the arrival delay time is increased, the departure delay time tends to increase.

In summary, online boarding, inflight entertainment/wifi, arrival/departure delay, and seat comfort were the most critical factors affecting airline passenger satisfaction levels. Loyal customers and customers with the Business class tended to have more satisfaction with airline services than others. This could be related to a variety of benefits that airlines offered to premium customers. In order to increase the satisfaction level of airline passengers, reducing the delay time of arrival/departure could be essential. In terms of the onboarding process, better access and usability of mobile apps and airline websites would promote customers' satisfaction. For the onboard experience, access to various entertainment sources with quality wifi service at a reasonable price would increase passenger satisfaction.

TABLEAU DASHBOARD AND DATA STORYTELLING

GOAL

The purpose of this dashboard is to provide a forum for discussion and analysis that can be easily understood by stakeholders on the significant factors associated with airline delays.

AUDIENCE

This dashboard's primary audience could be airline business stakeholders, quality analysts, schedule managers, airline employees, marketing managers, and more.

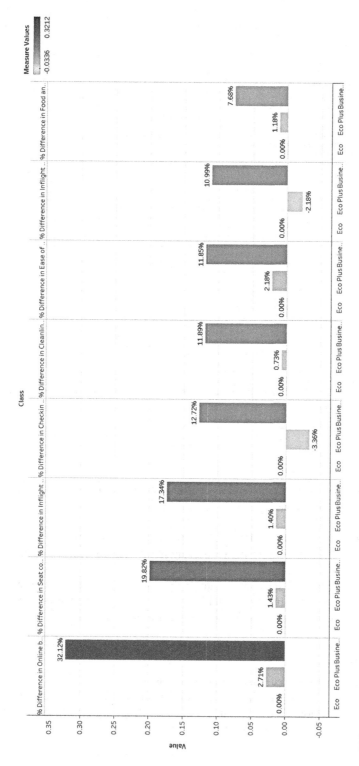

FIGURE 4.10 Bar charts of multiple satisfaction measures (percentage difference relative to the Eco class).

Bar Charts of the Percent Difference In Delay

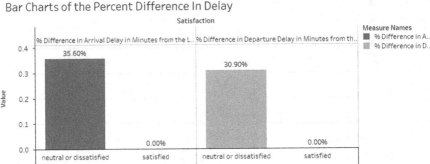

Scatter plot of Delay

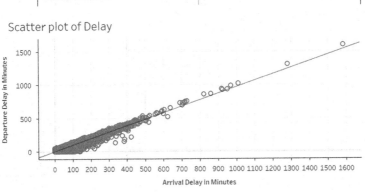

FIGURE 4.11   The dashboard of the bar charts and the scatter plot of the arrival and departure delay in minutes.

MESSAGE

Through the dashboard, stakeholders can think about the following questions and suggest specific solutions.

- How much does flight delay affect customer satisfaction?
- What is the relationship between delay in arrival and delay in departure?

Through the dashboard, it can more intuitively grasp the association between airline delays and customer satisfaction, and based on this, it can derive comprehensive quality improvement measures of many stakeholders.

ENGAGEMENT

Dashboards can be shared with airline delay quality analysts' offices for real-time status analysis. Airline managers can quickly identify daily carrier delays and customer satisfaction trends through cloud access from private offices.

4.4   DRIVERLESS CAR FAILURE (CASE 3)

4.4.1   INTRODUCTION OF DATASET

The driverless car has been gained a lot of attention and actual demand. The quality or safety of the autopilot is a vital factor for the drivers and passengers. In 2014 and 2015, seven driverless vehicles developing companies (Bosh, Delphi Automotive Systems, Google, Nissan, Mercedes-Benz, Tesla Motors, and Volkswagen) tested their driverless vehicles on the streets of the Golden State in California. Their testing results were required by law in California at that time.

During the autopilot test, drivers counted the number of disengagements. The disengagement meant the moment when drivers had to take control of the vehicle. This could be related to several factors such as drivers' fear, software error, severe weather conditions, and vague lane markings.

Table 4.5 shows the example data set. The full data could be assessed in the Appendix. Each month, total driving distance (miles) was tested, and each manufacturer measured the number of disengagements. Since there was a high variation of the driving distance across manufacturers, the number of disengagements per 10 miles was also considered for fair comparisons. Since Tesla reported "zero" disengagements throughout the test, Tesla's data was not evaluated in this study. There were several questions to be answered by analyzing these data.

Questions

- Which manufacturer tends to show better autopilot performance than other manufacturers?
- What is the variation of autopilot performance across manufacturers?

TABLE 4.5
The Example of the Autopilot Test Results during 2014–2015

Manufacturer	Month	Number of Disengagement	Autonomous Miles on Public Roads	Number of Disengagement per 10 miles
Google	2014/09	0	4207.2	0.00
Google	2014/10	14	23971.1	0.01
Google	2014/11	14	15836.6	0.01
Google	2014/12	40	9413.1	0.04
Google	2015/01	48	18192.1	0.03
Google	2015/02	12	18745.1	0.01
Google	2015/03	26	22204.2	0.01
Google	2015/04	47	31927.3	0.01
Google	2015/05	9	38016.8	0.00
Google	2015/06	7	42046.6	0.00

- What is the relationship between driving distance and the number of disengagements?
- Is the performance of autopilot changed over time?

4.4.2 TABLEAU EXAMPLE

To answer the first question (which manufacturer tends to show better autopilot performance than other manufacturers?), the bar charts were created as seen in Figure 4.12. Over 15 months, Google achieved a much higher driving distance compared to other manufacturers. For the number of disengagements per 10 miles, Google showed the lowest value among the six manufacturers. This indicates that Google showed the best performance of autonomous vehicles during the test.

For the second question (what is the variation of autopilot performance across manufacturers?), the box plot wax constructed as seen in Figure 4.13. Google and Volkswagen showed the lowest variability of the number of disengagements per 10 miles. Mercedes-Benz revealed the most considerable variability. Low variability could suggest the autopilot's consistent performance regardless of the different

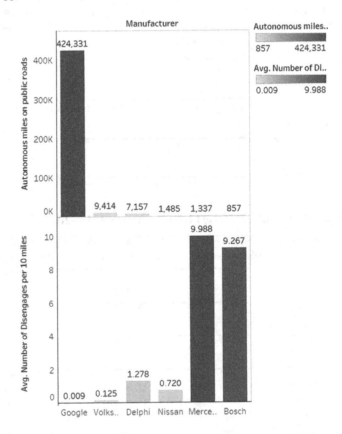

FIGURE 4.12 The bar charts of the driving distance and the number of disengagements per 10 miles.

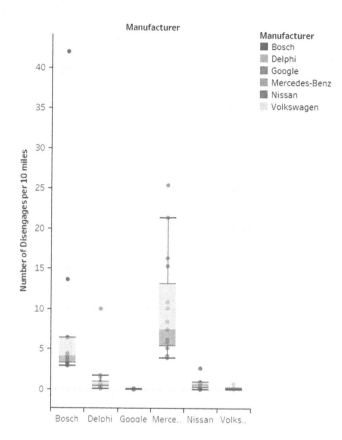

FIGURE 4.13   The box plot of the number of disengagements per 10 miles by manufacturers.

environments such as weather conditions and lane markings. This could be a good indicator of the robustness and reliability of autonomous cars.

The scatter plot was constructed to address the third question (what is the relationship between the driving distance and the number of disengagements?) as seen in Figure 4.14. Google showed a consistent number of disengagements regardless of driving distance, which was different from other manufacturers. Mercedes-Benz and Bosch showed the highest slope. It means that the number of disengagements was strongly increased as the driving distance increased. Besides Google, other manufacturers showed a positive linear relationship between the driving distance and the number of disengagements.

For the last question to be answered (is the performance of autopilot changed over time?), line charts were developed as seen in Figures 4.15 and 4.16. Google and Volkswagen showed a consistent number of disengagements per 10 miles throughout 15 months (Figure 4.15). Mercedes-Bens showed the highest fluctuation of the number of disengagements per 10 miles over time (Figure 4.15).

When we look at the line chart of the driving distance (Figure 4.16), Google showed a gradual increase in total driving distance over time. Volkswagen and Delphi showed some peak driving distance over a certain period.

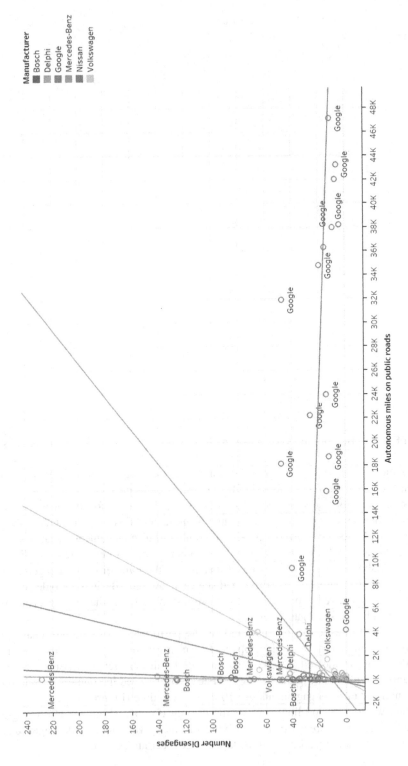

FIGURE 4.14   The scatter plot of driving distance and the number of disengagements by manufacturers.

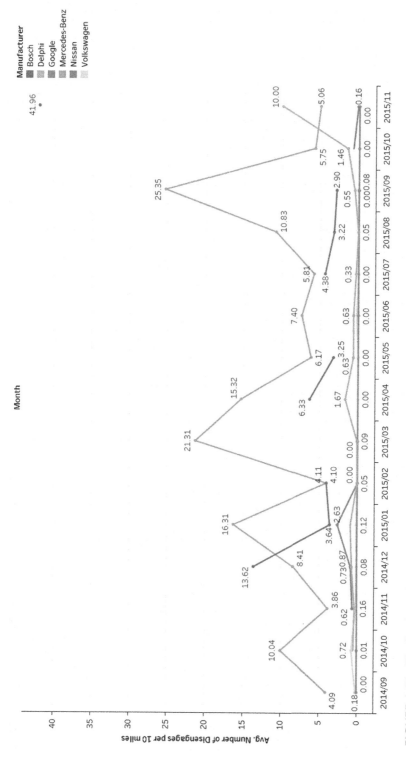

FIGURE 4.15   The lin chart of the number of disengagements per 10 miles over time.

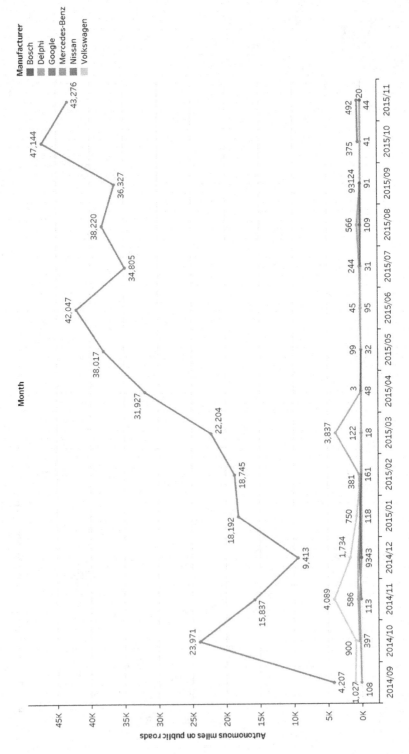

FIGURE 4.16 The lin chart of driving distance over time.

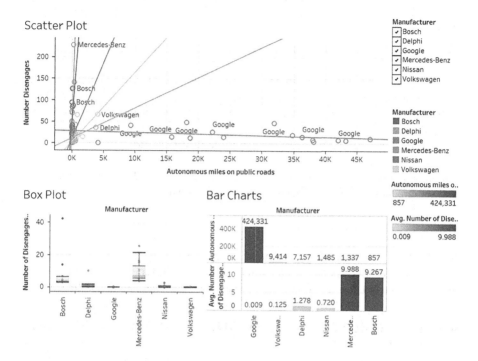

FIGURE 4.17   The quality dashboard of driverless car failure.

The dashboard was created as seen in Figure 4.17. This consists of the scatter plot, box plot, and vertical bar charts. In summary, Google showed the longest driving distance, the lowest number, and variability of disengagements per 10 miles, and its performance was consistent and robust throughout 15 months. There was high variability of autopilot performance among manufacturers. This indicated that autopilot's technology readiness was still at an early stage (based on 2014–2015 data). There were many rooms to be improved to ensure the safety of drivers and passengers.

TABLEAU DASHBOARD AND DATA STORYTELLING

Goal

This dashboard makes it easy to compare and understand how driverless vehicle performance varies by manufacturer.

Audience

The audience for the dashboard includes driverless vehicle manufacturers, quality analysts, reliability analysts, and marketers.

MESSAGE

Through dashboard analysis, stakeholders can get answers to the following questions.

- What is the difference in the performance of driverless vehicles by the manufacturer?
- How does the performance of driverless vehicles change according to the mileage?
- How consistent is the performance of the driverless car?

Through dashboard analysis, stakeholders can discuss potential answers to questions and set directions for future driverless vehicle performance improvement methods.

ENGAGEMENT

Stakeholders of each manufacturer can easily understand and analyze the differences in performance from competitors through this dashboard. Driverless vehicle developers and quality analysts can prioritize improvement directions through the dashboard.

4.5 REAL TIME VOICE CALL QUALITY DATA FROM CUSTOMERS (CASE 4)

4.5.1 INTRODUCTION OF DATASET

Since 2000, mobile phones have spread rapidly, and since 2010, many people use data communication through smartphones. Voice communication is the most basic service in the mobile communication business and understanding the quality and the performance of voice calls is critical to ensuring great customer experiences. Bad call experiences lead to frustrated customers, lost customer relationships, and have a real financial impact on businesses. However, measuring call quality was not an easy part for mobile carriers since users' subjective factors are reflected a lot. Thus, mobile communication companies have used customer survey techniques to check call quality, continue to monitor, and trace call performance to improve service quality based on the survey data.

The data set in this case captures the Customers Feedback using the MyCAll App developed by TRAI (Telecom regulatory authority of India) which is a statutory body set up by the Government of India. Its mission is to create and nurture conditions for the growth of telecommunications in India to enable the country to have a leading role in the emerging global information society. People faced a lot of issues due to low voice call quality and inability to express their opinion on a centralized platform in India. Indian government developed the MyCall app, which provides a platform to all telecom subscribers in India to voice their opinion about their call quality, including call drop, and provide feedback to TRAI. This feedback helps TRAI analyze service providers' performance and put the same in the public domain to make an informed decision while choosing their service provider.

The data is captured for various service providers in India, at multiple locations, network types 2G, 3G, 4G, ratings, coordinates, etc. Customers rate their experience

TABLE 4.6

The Variable and Description of the Voice Call Quality Data

Variable	Description
Operator	Telecom service provider
Indoor_Outdoor_Travelling	The location status information when users rate service quality
Network Type	The type of Network and standard for telecommunication
Rating	Quality rated by customers (0: lowest quality; 5: highest quality)
Call Drop Category	Reported data If a call is dropped (call drop issue)
Latitude	Geographic coordinate located when the quality was rated
Longitude	Geographic coordinate located when the quality was rated
State Name	Location information

with voice call quality in real-time and help TRAI gather customer experience data along with Network data.

The full data set is available in Kaggle (https://www.kaggle.com/pranaysharma1108/ real-time-voice-call-quality-data-from-customers). Table 4.7 shows the example of the partial data set including several properties and the quality rating.

Questions

- What is the distribution of call quality?
- What is the level of overall call quality? (by the operator, by region, by the network)
- Based on the analysis results, what are the suggestions to improve call quality?

4.5.2 TABLEAU EXAMPLE

To address the first question (what is the distribution of call quality?), the histogram was constructed to see the distributed overview of call quality ratings (1 through 5). As seen in Figure 4.18, the majority of the call quality was distributed between 4 and 5. However, it was noted that there was a significant number of calls (11,708) rated "1" that could be categorized as bad quality. This shows that lots of customers still faced call quality issues and inconvenience so operators should improve the quality issues for customer experience.

To answer the second question (What is the level of overall call quality by the operator, by region, by the network?), the vertical bar chart and map chart were created to see the overviews of call quality among regions, operators, the type of network, and the quality rating.

Average Call Quality Rate per Operator

Based on the analysis except for the data marked as "Others" operator, 7 out of 9 operators listed show over average call quality (3.078) but the remaining two operators show below average call quality (Figure 4.19). This chart shows that one

TABLE 4.7

Example Data of Quality Rating

Operator	Indoor Outdoor Traveling	Network Type	Rating	Call Drop Category	Latitude	Longitude	State Name
Airtel	Indoor	3G	5	Satisfactory	28.42296647	76.91232449	Haryana
RJio	Indoor	4G	4	Satisfactory	11.15835753	77.30189698	Tamil Nadu
Airtel	Outdoor	3G	5	Satisfactory	28.42293129	76.91225267	Haryana
Airtel	Traveling	3G	5	Satisfactory	28.42294679	76.91226046	Haryana
RJio	Indoor	4G	5	Satisfactory	25.62598952	85.0942942	Bihar
RJio	Traveling	4G	4	Satisfactory	14.91332118	79.9937972	Andhra Pradesh
Airtel	Traveling	4G	1	Satisfactory	19.9373255	73.53618993	Maharashtra
RJio	Outdoor	4G	4	Satisfactory	26.89203316	75.7257245	Rajasthan
RJio	Indoor	4G	5	Satisfactory	20.28782899	85.86483224	Odisha
RJio	Indoor	4G	2	Satisfactory	9.426250956	77.80240493	Tamil Nadu
Idea	Outdoor	Unknown	4	Satisfactory	−1	−1	
RJio	Indoor	4G	5	Satisfactory	25.62596263	85.09411065	Bihar
Airtel	Outdoor	4G	5	Satisfactory	26.78134153	82.15096136	Uttar Pradesh
BSNL	Indoor	3G	1	Poor Network	−1	−1	

* If Latitude and Longitude are −1 or 0 or any out of India geography, it usually happens when an android user or apple user blocked the App to accesses their location or Android Apis which google provides are unable to capture coordinate information.

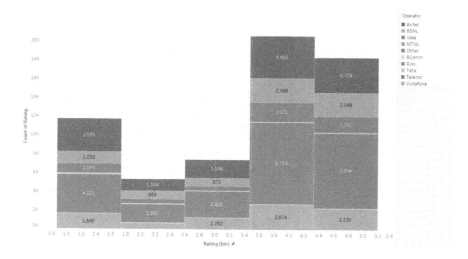

FIGURE 4.18 Histogram of the distributed overview of call quality ratings.

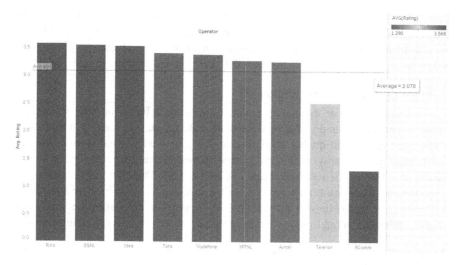

FIGURE 4.19 Vertical bar chart of average call quality rate per operator.

operator (RComm) has bad call quality (under 1.5), especially with other operators. To compete with service providers in the market, this operator should improve the quality issues soon since this is an obtrusive difference.

Average Quality Rate per Region (1)

To observe call quality geographically over nationwide, the Map chart could be constructed using Latitude and Longitude columns on the data set (Figure 4.20). According to the Map chart, there was no specific geographical pattern or trend to

FIGURE 4.20   Map chart to observe call quality geographically over nationwide.

conclude that call quality was determined based on regional location. However, this Map chart could be a useful tool and overview at a glance regarding which region would show a quality issue in the future and improve the problems (e.g., operators should expand infrastructure to enhance the quality issue for specific states or cities).

Average Quality Rate per Region (2)

To observe and evaluate the quality level per each state in India, the vertical bar chart could be constructed and sorted by the average rate per state to identify which states show good or bad call quality level (Figure 4.21). Overall, around 7 states showed outstanding good quality with above rate 4. However, customers in 2 states were facing very bad experiences (under rate 2) in call quality. This chart could not provide more details for the root cause analysis of the bad quality issue in these states with low rates due to the limited information. To improve these issues, operators and related authorities should take action based on detailed analysis and scrutinization.

Average Quality Rate per Network

To check the relationship between the call quality and the network type, the vertical bar chart was created and sorted based on the quality rate (Figure 4.22). To estimate the correlation between the two factors, it was confirmed that the call quality evaluation increased from 2G, 3G to 4G except for the case where the network type was not provided in the data set. This is the expected result since the newer generation is faster, more secure, and more reliable assuming that other factors are the same

For the last question (Based on the analysis results, what are the suggestions to improve call quality?), we could think about ways to enhance the quality of call based on the data collected and the analysis above. The quality dashboard of call quality was created to provide a holistic and comprehensive overview of the measures seen in Figure 4.23.

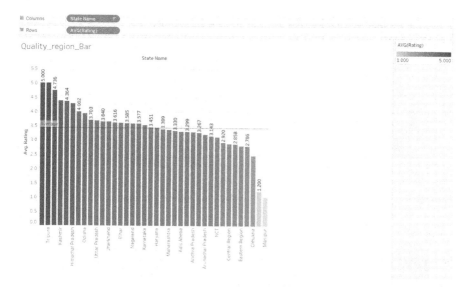

FIGURE 4.21 The vertical bar chart of the quality level per each state in India.

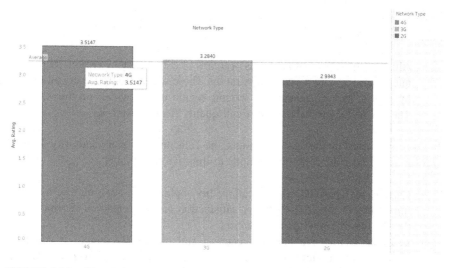

FIGURE 4.22 The vertical bar chart showing the relationship between the call quality and the network type.

- The overall high level of call quality between 4 and 5 was shown, but it can be seen that still many customers were not satisfied with some bad quality.
- There was a difference in call quality for each service provider, which was characterized by the quality of a specific service provider (RComm) showing lower call quality than other service providers.

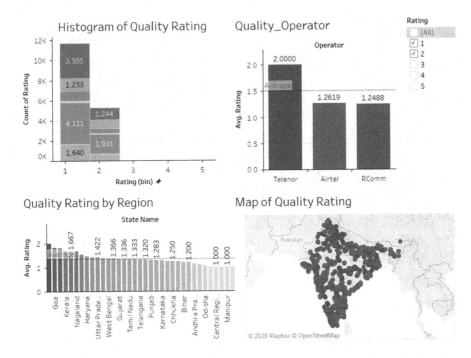

FIGURE 4.23   The call quality dashboard.

- Although there were no patterns or trends of call quality by region, there were many regions with a two or less rating. There was a difference in call quality by region, and customers in a specific region used low call service.
- The 2G had significantly lower call quality than 4G and 3G.

In summary, based on the analysis results, the Telecom regulatory authority of India (TRAI) could take the following actions to improve call quality.

- Carriers with particularly low call quality could order or recommend a quality improvement. Overall customer satisfaction can be improved by improving the quality of some specific carriers.
- In order to improve the difference in call quality by region, it could be identified the regions with low call quality, analyze the root cause, and conduct call quality improvement activities such as expanding infrastructure.
- Replace equipment or facilities that have undergone aging, including 2G networks, and upgrade to the next-generation network as a whole.

TABLEAU DASHBOARD AND DATA STORYTELLING

GOAL

This dashboard aims to provide stakeholders call quality feedback collected via MyCAll App at a glance.

AUDIENCE

The primary audience will be an official and staff of the TRAI, responsible for monitoring customer complaints and resolving issues.

MESSAGE

We would get the following answers through the dashboard. Through the identified data, operators, and regions with low call quality are identified, then appropriate actions will be taken for quality improvement methods are found.

- Which operators provide low-value services?
- What is the frequency of poor quality calls?
- What is the level of call quality by region?

ENGAGEMENT

Data collected by MyCAll App will be aggregated in real-time and displayed through a dashboard. India's telecom regulatory authority (TRAI)'s control room will use this dashboard to monitor call quality and periodically share relevant information via email with stakeholders.

4.6 BREWERY PRODUCTION (CASE 5)

4.6.1 INTRODUCTION OF DATASET

Beer has been one of the preferred beverages over the past decades in the US. Based on the Gallup Poll, 2019, beer has been consistently showing greater preference than wine and spirits. By reflecting this preference, beer production and distribution are essential factors in the US beer industry. The U.S. Department of the Treasury (Alcohol and Tobacco Tax and Trade Bureau) reports the beer statistics annually. This data could be helpful to understand the trends of brewery production over the years.

Table 4.8 shows the sample data set, which was retrieved from the website (https://www.ttb.gov/beer/statistics). Here are the explanations of the variables.

- Barrels (31 gallons): The production size is based on annual production by each brewer.
- The number of breweries: Number of breweries reporting production and paid taxes during the calendar year.
- Total barrels: The total number of barrels produced.
- Taxable Removals: The number of barrels subject to tax by the breweries.
- Percentage of taxable removals: The proportion of the taxable removals out of total barrels.
- Total shipped (exported): The number of total barrels without payment of tax for direct export.

TABLE 4.8
The Sample Data Set of the Brewery Production

Year	Barrels (31 gallons)	Number of Breweries	Total Barrels	Taxable Removals	Percentage of Taxable Removals	Total Shipped (Exported)
2008	6,000,001 Barrels and Over	11	121637275.3	113249020.3	93.1038779	1567327.27
2008	1,000,001 to 6,000,000 Barrels (5)	9	60822125.25	56064453.82	92.17772906	2170988.71
2008	500,001 to 1,000,000 Barrels	7	4881373.45	4299799.29	88.0858499	49987.21
2008	100,001 to 500,000 Barrels	30	7064945.49	6151586.6	87.07196126	262872.84
2008	60,001 to 100,000 Barrels	20	1587136.1	1331836.9	83.91447337	5626.56
2008	30,001 to 60,000 Barrels	26	1162296.26	1055970.16	90.85206555	12641.63
2008	15,001 to 30,000 Barrels	43	895640.53	765924.75	85.51698191	1138.74
2008	7,501 to 15,000 Barrels	40	422694.05	327582.03	77.49861395	15888.96
2008	1,001 to 7,500 Barrels	360	851718.37	750998.94	88.17456174	10738.76
2008	1 to 1,000 Barrels	979	381660.76	350441.12	91.82005507	252.03
2008	Under 1 Barrel	163	0.67	7725.03	1152989.552	166.68
2008	Total	1688	199706866.3	184355339	92.31296971	4097629.39
2009	6,000,001 Barrels and Over	18	171232881.6	159643984.2	93.23208413	3639970.11
2009	1,000,001 to 6,000,000 Barrels (5)	4	9970404.28	9592722.75	96.21197376	14548.37
2009	500,001 to 1,000,000 Barrels	7	4831385.68	4535659.48	93.87906039	21563.66

Here are the questions that we may answer from the data analysis.

Questions

- What is the distribution of the number of breweries by different production (barrels) sizes?
- What is the trend of the number of breweries and total barrels over time?

- What is the distribution of total shipped by different production (barrels) sizes?
- What is the difference in the percentage of taxable removals by production (barrels) size?

4.6.2 TABLEAU EXAMPLE

To answer the first question (What is the distribution of the number of breweries by different production (barrels) sizes?), the Pareto chart could be considered as seen in Figure 4.24. It shows that the production (barrels) size of 1 to 1,000 barrels and 1,001 to 7,500 barrels consist of 87.08% of the total number of breweries. This suggests that this production size (1 to 7,500 barrels) is most common by breweries.

For the second question (What is a trend of the number of breweries and total barrels over time?), the line chars could be considered. For the number of breweries, there has been a dramatic increase since 2008. Year 2019s number of breweries is about four times higher than the one in 2008. On the other hand, the number of total barrels showed the opposite trend. There was a gradually decreasing trend of the total barrels over time. This indicates that each brewery tends to produce a lower number of total barrels over time (Figure 4.25).

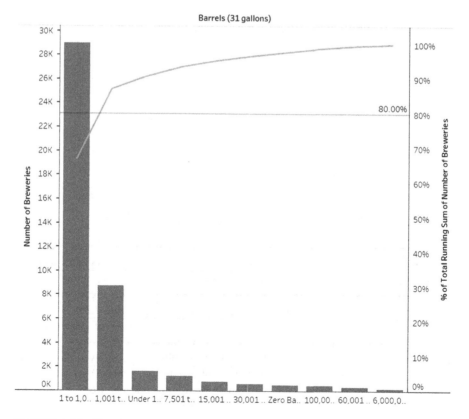

FIGURE 4.24 The Pareto chart of the number of breweries by production (barrels) size.

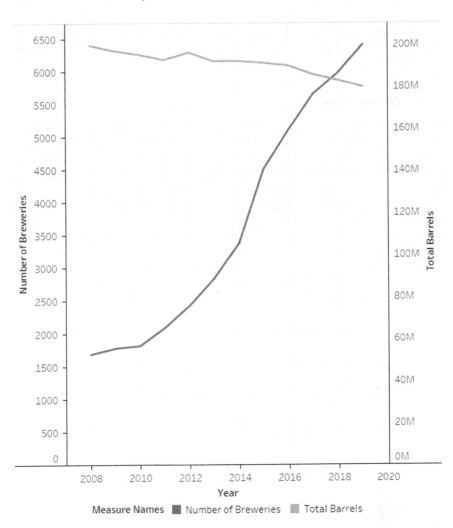

FIGURE 4.25   The line chart of the number of breweries and total barrels.

The pie chart could be considered to address the third question (What is the distribution of total shipped by different production (barrels) size?). It shows that 6,000,001 barrels and overproduction size showed the highest proportion (79.74%) of total shipped (Exported) followed by 2,000,000 to 6,000,000 barrels (8.18%). This suggests that mass production of the beer typically targets direct export shipping (Figure 4.26).

For the last question to be answered (What is the difference of percentage of taxable removals by production (barrels) size?), the vertical bar chart could be considered. The production size 1,000,001 to 1,999,999 barrels showed the highest percentage of taxable removals (98.57%) followed by 2,000,000 to 6,000,000 barrels (96.85%). Typically, greater than 90% of total barrels were counted as taxable removals (Figure 4.27).

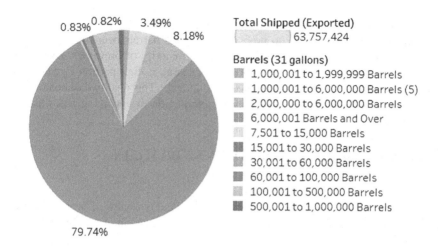

FIGURE 4.26   The pie chart of total shipped by production (barrels) size.

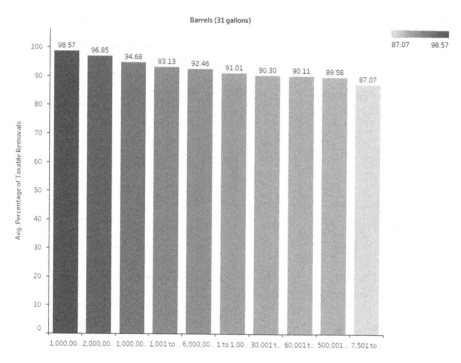

FIGURE 4.27   The vertical bar chart of taxable removals by production (barrels) size.

The quality dashboard of brewery production was created to have a comprehensive analysis of the brewery data. The filtering of year was allowed to see the change of plots over a specific period of time. In summary, barrels' mass-production typically targets direct export shipments to meet customers' great needs worldwide.

Over the last 10 years, there has been a dramatic increase in the number of breweries whereas each brewery tended to produce fewer total barrels over time. This is associated with the Pareto chart showing that the majority of breweries (over 80%) produced small size barrels (1 to 7,500). In general, a high portion (greater than 90%) of total barrels was considered taxable removals. This quality dashboard could be useful to monitor the trends of brewery production in upcoming years as well (Figure 4.28).

TABLEAU DASHBOARD AND DATA STORYTELLING

GOAL

This dashboard aims to provide an easy-to-understand overview of beer production and related indicators each year based on information from the U.S. Department of the Treasury.

AUDIENCE

Stakeholders and quality analysts interested in beer production and import or export could be a potential audience.

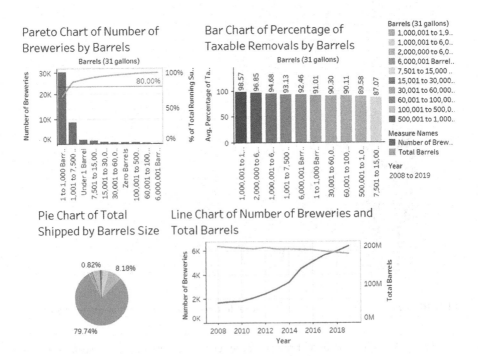

FIGURE 4.28   The quality dashboard of brewery production.

MESSAGE

Through the information on the dashboard, stakeholders can effectively get answers to the following questions.

- How is beer production changing every year?
- How do beer exports relate to the production scale of beer manufacturers?

Various dashboard indicators can provide specific information about the question and predict future US beer production.

ENGAGEMENT

By checking the dashboard annually for beer producers, they can understand production trends and react quickly to new changes. Beer-related export managers can make reasonable predictions about future exports through the dashboard.

4.7 SEOUL BIKE SHARING DEMAND (CASE 6)

4.7.1 INTRODUCTION OF DATASET

Rental bikes have gained more popularity these days due to their flexibility, mobility, low cost, and health benefits in urban cities. Understanding the demand for rental bikes is essential to estimate rental bikes' availability over various time periods and locations. Demand information can also help to allocate the optimal amount of supply of rental bikes. These factors could be critically related to customer satisfaction and traffic. The original dataset is obtained from South Korea Public Holidays (http://data.seoul.go.kr/) and a specific dataset from 2017 to 2018 can be obtained from the machine learning repository website at the University of California Irvine (https://archive.ics.uci.edu/ml/datasets/Seoul+Bike+Sharing+Demand). Table 4.9 shows the sample dataset and here are the explanations of each variable.

- Date: Year – Month – Day
- Rented Bike Count: number of bokes rented per hour
- Temperature: Temperature in Celsius
- Rainfall: Rainfall in mm
- Seasons: Winter, Spring, Summer, and Autumn
- Holiday: Holiday and no holiday

Here are the questions that we could explore through the data analysis.

Questions

- What is the trend of rented bike count over the months?
- Which seasons show greater demand for the rented bike than other seasons?

TABLE 4.9
The Sample Data Set of Seoul Bike Sharing Demand

Date	Rented Bike Count	Temperature	Rainfall	Seasons	Holiday
1/12/2017	254	−5.2	0	Winter	No Holiday
1/12/2017	204	−5.5	0	Winter	No Holiday
1/12/2017	173	−6	0	Winter	No Holiday
1/12/2017	107	−6.2	0	Winter	No Holiday
1/12/2017	78	−6	0	Winter	No Holiday
1/12/2017	100	−6.4	0	Winter	No Holiday
1/12/2017	181	−6.6	0	Winter	No Holiday
1/12/2017	460	−7.4	0	Winter	No Holiday
1/12/2017	930	−7.6	0	Winter	No Holiday
1/12/2017	490	−6.5	0	Winter	No Holiday
1/12/2017	339	−3.5	0	Winter	No Holiday
1/12/2017	360	−0.5	0	Winter	No Holiday
1/12/2017	449	1.7	0	Winter	No Holiday
1/12/2017	451	2.4	0	Winter	No Holiday
1/12/2017	447	3	0	Winter	No Holiday

- Is the demand for rented bikes affected by the holiday season?
- Is there a relationship between the rented bike demand and temperature?
- Is there a relationship between the rented bike demand and the amount of rainfall?

4.7.2 TABLEAU EXAMPLE

To answer the first question (What is the trend of rented bike count over the months?), the line chart could be considered as seen in Figure 4.29. It shows that there is a significant change in rented bike count over the months. From February, the demand for the rented bike has continuously increased until June. After that, the decreasing trend of the rented bike was shown. This trend was similar to the trend of temperature over the months.

To answer the second question (Which seasons show greater demand for rented bike than other seasons?), the pie chart could be considered as seen in Figure 4.30. The summer shows the highest demand for the rented bike (37%), followed by Autumn (29%). As expected, Winter showed the lowest demand (7.9%). It suggests that the supply of the rented bikes could be differently allocated by various seasons.

To answer the third question (Is demand for rented bikes affected by a holiday season?), the stacked bar chart could be considered as seen in Figure 4.31. It shows that no holiday had a 1.4 times greater demand for the rented bike than a holiday season. This suggests that some of the customers used rented bikes for their commute to jobs.

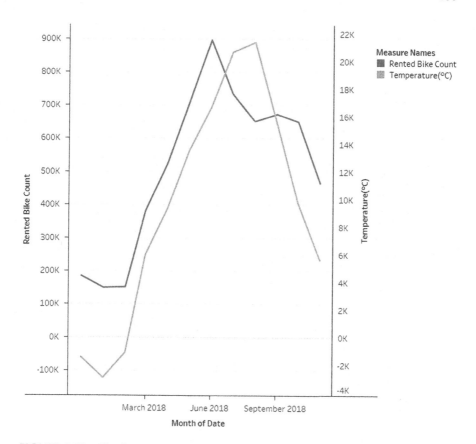

FIGURE 4.29 The line charts of rented bike count and temperature over the months.

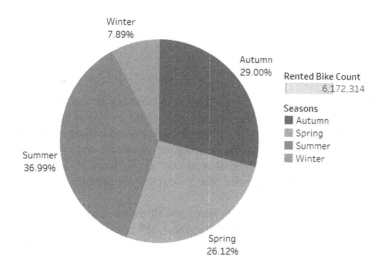

FIGURE 4.30 The pie chart of rented bike count by seasons.

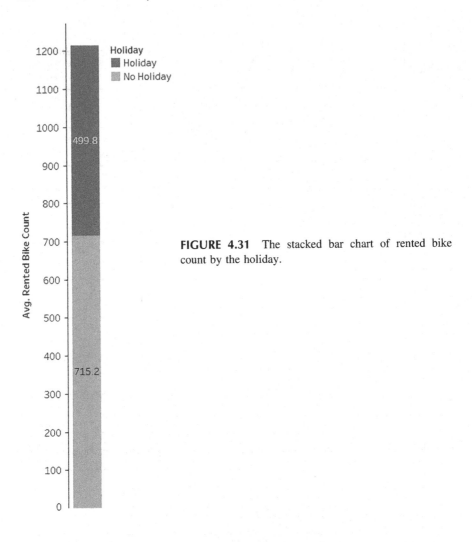

FIGURE 4.31 The stacked bar chart of rented bike count by the holiday.

To answer the fourth question (Is there a relationship between the rented bike demand and temperature?), the scatter plot could be considered as seen in Figure 4.32. It shows that a positive relationship existed between the rented bike count and the temperature. As the temperature increased, the rented bike count tended to grow as well. However, after around 25 °C, the rented bike count substantially decreased. This indicates that too high a temperature could reduce the demand for rented bikes.

To answer the fifth question (Is there a relationship between the rented bike demand and the amount of rainfall?), the scatter plot could be considered as seen in Figure 4.33. It shows that the greatest bike demand existed with no rainfall. As the amount of rainfall increased, the demand for rented bike dramatically decreased as a

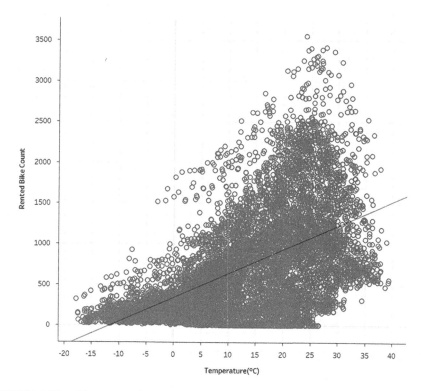

FIGURE 4.32   The scatter plot of rented bike count and temperature.

nonlinear trend. It suggests that the rainy weather condition is a critical factor affecting rented bike demand per day.

The quality dashboard of Seoul bike sharing demand was creased as seen in Figure 4.34. This consists of line plots, a pie chart, and a stacked bar chart. Filtering option of Month, Year of Date allows interpreting the change of rented bike over the month.

TABLEAU DASHBOARD AND DATA STORYTELLING

GOAL

This dashboard aims to understand Seoul's bike demand and adjust the appropriate bike supply to increase customer satisfaction.

AUDIENCE

Dashboard audiences could include bike rental stakeholders, bike rental app developers, quality analysts, and marketing experts.

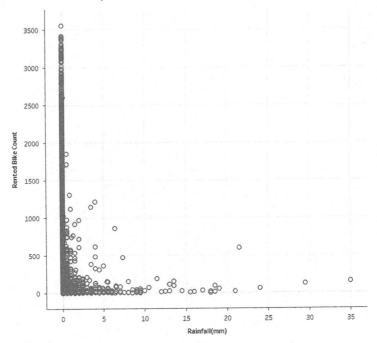

FIGURE 4.33   The scatter plot of rented bike count and rainfall.

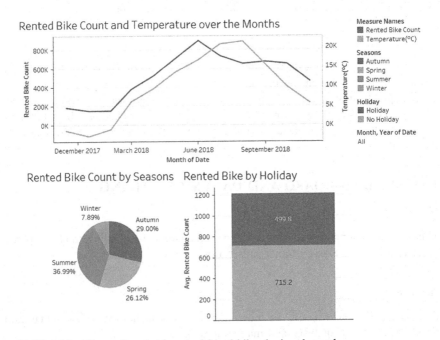

FIGURE 4.34   The quality dashboard of Seoul bike sharing demand.

Message

Through the dashboard analysis, stakeholders can think of the following questions and find solutions to them.

- Does the demand for bicycle rental vary by season?
- What is the difference between the monthly demand for bike rental?
- Is the demand for bike rental affected by holidays?

Through the dashboard, stakeholders can get specific information about the above questions and make more rational decisions.

Engagement

Bicycle rental companies can monitor this dashboard to predict the rented bikes' demand and find appropriate countermeasures.

REFERENCE

Cortez, P., Cerdeira, A., Almeida, F., Matos, T., & Reis, J. (2009). Modeling wine preferences by data mining from physicochemical properties. *Decision Support Systems*, *47*(4), 547–553

Index

Printed in the United States
by Baker & Taylor Publisher Services